APOCALYPTIC LITERATURE

Study by Marc Jolley
Commentary by Cecil Sherman

Free downloadable Teaching Guide for this study available at
NextSunday.com/teachingguides

NextSunday Resources
6316 Peake Road
Macon, Georgia 31210-3960
1-800-747-3016
©2012 by NextSunday Resources
All rights reserved.
Printed in the United States of America.

Library of Congress Cataloging-in-Publication Data

CIP Information on file.

TABLE OF CONTENTS

Apocalyptic Literature

HOW TO USE THIS STUDY

NextSunday Resources Adult Bible Studies are designed to help adults study Scripture seriously within the context of the larger Christian tradition and, through that process, find their faith renewed, challenged, and strengthened. We study the Scriptures because we believe they affect our current lives in important ways. Each study contains the following three components:

Study Guide

Each study guide lesson is arranged in four movements:

Remembering provides a frame of reference for the Scriptures.

Studying is centered on giving the biblical material in-depth attention while often surrounding it with helpful insights from theology, ethics, church history, and other areas.

Understanding helps us find relevant connections between our lives and the biblical message.

What About Me? provides brief statements that help unite life issues with the meaning of the biblical text.

Commentary

Each study guide lesson is accompanied by an additional, in-depth commentary on the biblical material. Written by a different author than the study guide, each commentary gives the opportunity for learners to approach the Scripture text from a separate but complementary viewpointt.

Teaching Guide

In addition to the provided study guide and commentary, *NextSunday Resources* also provides a *free* downloadable teaching guide, available at NextSunday.com. Each teaching guide gives the teacher tools for focusing on the content of each study guide lesson through additional commentary and Bible background information. Through teacher helps and teaching options, each teaching guide also provides substance for variety and choice in the preparation of each lesson.

NextSunday
Resources

STUDY INTRODUCTION

2012 marks the year some believe the ancient Mayans predicted the end of this world. In 2011, American Christian radio host Harold Camping predicted the end of the world would take place that year. The Y2K scare leading up to the year 2000 brought predictions and prophecies of impending disaster.

Since the first prophets and soothsayers from the ancient Near East, prophecies and predictions of the end of the world have threaded their way into the human fabric. Between the time of the restoration of the temple (early fifth century BC) and today, myriads of writers, prophets, and dreamers have shared their visions of God's ultimate conquering of the world. However, this phenomenon was never more popular than between the third century BC until the second century AD.

During this period, among the Jews and Christians, a kind of literature existed that we describe as "apocalyptic." The word "apocalypse" refers to things hidden, or secrets to be revealed. It is also the title of John's book known as Revelation.

Is this literature about the future? Regarding Daniel and Revelation, many believe that the answer is yes. In fact, many people spend their entire lives trying to figure out whether these books foretell the end of the world. This is, however, neither the purpose nor the style of apocalyptic literature. Its purpose surrounds the present, not the future.

Let's consider the book of Daniel for its style. The author lived around 167–164 BC and compiled the book using old tales of a prophet named Daniel from the sixth century (chapters 1–6). He then composed chapters 7–12 as if Daniel had written them himself 400 years earlier. Because the original audience was familiar with this technique of writing, using the name of a hero from the past, the method was not deceptive—and certainly not intentionally so. The writings have been hidden in secret until the right time: 167–164 BC—conveniently, the time of the author. The author writes to an audience of his own day and time about the events of persecution and trial he and his contemporaries are facing, as well as how those times were "prophesied" hundreds of years ago. Using wild imagery like beasts, monsters, divine beings, and a famous hero from the past (Daniel), the author relays how God will conquer these enemies. The faithful will experience possible death and certain persecution, but this much is certain: the victory will be God's.

This unit will examine five apocalyptic texts in the Bible. With each new year bringing a new prediction of impending doom, it is always a perfect time to get the story straight. Apocalyptic literature does not address the future. It addresses our present.

REASSURING THE FAITHFUL

Zechariah 12:1-10

Central Question

How are you assured that God is ultimately in control?

Scripture

Zechariah 12:1-10 An Oracle. The word of the LORD concerning Israel: Thus says the LORD, who stretched out the heavens and founded the earth and formed the human spirit within: 2 See, I am about to make Jerusalem a cup of reeling for all the surrounding peoples; it will be against Judah also in the siege against Jerusalem. 3 On that day I will make Jerusalem a heavy stone for all the peoples; all who lift it shall grievously hurt themselves. And all the nations of the earth shall come together against it. 4 On that day, says the LORD, I will strike every horse with panic, and its rider with madness. But on the house of Judah I will keep a watchful eye, when I strike every horse of the peoples with blindness. 5 Then the clans of Judah shall say to themselves, "The inhabitants of Jerusalem have strength through the LORD of hosts, their God." 6 On that day I will make the clans of Judah like a blazing pot on a pile of wood, like a flaming torch among sheaves; and they shall devour to the right and to the left all the surrounding peoples, while Jerusalem shall again be inhabited in its place, in Jerusalem. 7 And the LORD will give victory to the tents of Judah first, that the glory of the house of David and the glory of the inhabitants of Jerusalem may not be exalted over that of Judah. 8 On that day the LORD will shield the inhabitants of Jerusalem so that the feeblest among them on that day shall be like David, and the house of David shall be like God, like the angel of the LORD, at their head. 9 And on that day I will seek to destroy all the nations that come against Jerusalem. 10 And I will pour out a spirit of compassion and supplication on the house of David and the inhabitants of Jerusalem, so that, when they look on the one whom they have pierced, they shall mourn for him, as one mourns for an only child, and weep bitterly over him, as one weeps over a firstborn.

Remembering

The prophet Zechariah preached God's Word both during and after the restoration of Jerusalem (after 538 BC). His message was one of encouragement to the faithful, yet was also about each individual's need to keep the commandments of God in their daily lives. Only such obedience to God could prevent another exile. According to the prophets and the writers of Joshua through Kings, the Exile was God's punishment of the people for their disobedience and idolatry. Now the prophet Zechariah asked the people to have faith in God—the *true* king—not in the power of the State.

The book of Zechariah is divided into two parts: chapters 1–8 and chapters 9–14. Understanding why this division exists is significant for us as modern readers. At first glance, the two parts appear to be in tension with one another, but a closer reading reveals the dependency of one part on the other. Chapters 1–8 were written after the Babylonian Exile near the end of the sixth century, and chapters 9–14 were written by either a disciple or disciples of Zechariah in the next century. These latter chapters are full of figurative language and talk of the "day of the LORD" and God's "final" victory.

One of the prophet's most frequently used phrases in the last

The Babylonian Exile began in 598/7 BC when Nebuchadrezzar defeated the rebel forces of Jehoiakim. The end of the rebellion began the forced removal of the royal family, court officials, and the leading citizens of Judah to Babylon (see 2 Kgs 24:1-17). A second rebellion a few years later (587/6 BC) brought about the destruction of the temple in Jerusalem and another deportation of the people.

half of the book is "the day of the LORD." Popular with early apocalyptic literature (see unit introduction) and continually used by later writers, this phrase is often thought to be a reference to the end of the world. In truth, however, the prophets used this phrase in a much more relevant and relative manner: to indicate a great—and often horrible— intervention by God into the world's affairs. In verses 3-4 the prophet says, "On that day..." the LORD will bring judgment on the "house of Judah" (v. 4). The Jews had only *just* returned to the promised land after the Babylonian Exile, so what was this prophet talking about? If things had gone so well in the prior century, then why was the day of the LORD now so near? Why was judgment coming? Today's passage was undoubtedly significant to its first hearers, but it speaks just as loudly for us today.

The phrase "apocalyptic literature" refers to a group of writings that "reveal hidden information" (apocalyptic). This field of literature typically includes characteristics such as visions, the revelation of secrets, and the advent of a heavenly being who interprets the vision.

Studying

(12:1-5) Zechariah's prophetic word begins with an "Oracle," a term referring to the message of God delivered through a prophet or a priest. Common among oracles in the Old Testament—and a few in the New Testament (see 1 Cor 15:51; 2 Cor 12:9; 1 Thess 3:4)—was the focus on communicating an *immediate* concern to both the prophet and (hopefully) the recipients. Oracles were also generally accompanied by the characteristic phrase, "Thus says the Lord" (as in 12:1).

God is described in these opening verses as the one "who stretched out the heavens" and "founded the earth and formed the human spirit within." Both are affirmations of God's power and ability to carry out this oracle of impending disaster. God's Word is to be taken seriously and acted upon promptly.

In fact, of primary importance in apocalyptic literature is "the word of the LORD." When God speaks, the prophet *must* speak the message. When God speaks, people *must* listen. The phrase "thus says the LORD" is commonly used by the prophets, but its importance cannot be overestimated. As Barbara Brown Taylor says, "It is a sad thing in our society when 'scientific studies show' carries more authority than the phrase 'thus says the LORD.'" This assertion indicates that God— the same God who stretched out the heavens and founded the earth (Isa 42:5)—has a special word of utmost importance for the people. This is no idol made of clay or stone from the people's past, but the one true God.

According to the oracle, God is going to make Jerusalem a "cup of reeling for all the surrounding peoples." The "cup" in the Bible is a symbol of judgment (see Ps 75:8; Isa 11:6, 51:7; Jer 25:5; Mk 14:36). This oracle is no idle threat, but comes from the very God who created the universe and who has previously allowed exile to come as punishment.

Upon hearing the oracle, the people must have wondered frantically, "When is judgment coming? Against whom is it coming? Why will there be a siege against Jerusalem? Who will besiege the city?" The answers to these questions are found in verses 3-4. It will happen "on that day," a phrase used to signal God's intervention in history, usually in an extreme, often dreadful way. This time, however, it will not be a foreign enemy that lays siege against the walls of Jerusalem, but instead, it will be God. To make matters worse, God has even invited the surrounding nations to come and watch. Panic will strike every house and the rider will become mad.

In the second half of verse 4, we find a twist to the plot: "But on the house of Judah I will keep a watchful eye...." Is not God's judgment coming against Judah? This "confusion" is the splendor of apocalyptic writing. According to Zechariah, the "day of the LORD" would come between two factions of people in Jerusalem. One side, the "shepherds" of Israel (10:1-12), held control; the other side, the house of Judah, looked to the prophets for God's help. The struggle in Jerusalem was not with outsiders, but rather was internal. Longing to be released from the control of the religious elite (Hanson, *The Dawn of Apocalyptic*), the group that surrounded this prophet looked to "the day of the LORD" when their faith would emerge victorious.

From the study of eschatology (the study of the last days or final things), we learn that the "day of the LORD" was a way to speak about the day that God's judgment would set the balance and vindicate the righteous. This vindication was, of course, based on the repentance of the person or nation.

(12:6-10) "On that day" the "clans of Judah" will be punished, and the true inhabitants of Jerusalem—the house of Judah—will replace the controlling order. This internal conflict is not described in any detail. In fact, we know of no one on either side. What we *do* know, however, is that God is on the side of the prophet and the "house of David." "On that day" God will protect the "inhabitants of Jerusalem" against the religious elite who have caused the (unknown) trouble.

What appears to have been a religious dispute was significant enough at the time to warrant the prophet's taking sides. The one side identifies itself with the "house of David," and incidentally, was the side that produced this text. Upon those loyal to the "house of David," God would "pour out a spirit of compassion and supplication," so that when they looked on the "one whom *they* [the enemy; emphasis added] have pierced," they would be comforted. Exactly who this pierced one is we do not know. It is not a reference to Jesus, but to one who was pierced on the people's behalf.

Another text originating from the same time in Jerusalem, often thought to be a prophecy of the death of Jesus Christ, also makes reference to this unnamed individual (Isa 52:13–53:12). The Hebrew reads, "When they look on *me*"—not "the one" as in the New Revised Standard Version—"whom they have pierced." Since it is often difficult to determine whether the prophet speaks of himself or of God, we must conclude that the "pierced" one is either the literally persecuted prophet or the metaphorically "pierced" God. Either way, this allusion reveals an attack on

the community of faith, and the prophet's message is to comfort and assure the people that God is in control and that the faithful will survive by their faith.

Understanding

The division between the two groups in Jerusalem during the fifth century BC was neither the first nor the last in the history of the world. Religious history is riddled with schisms and disagreements.

Throughout Christian history there have been opposing factions over theology, practice, and issues of polity, with each side claiming to be doing God's will. During the American Civil War, Abraham Lincoln noted that both sides prayed to the same God and worshipped the same risen Savior. In this century many denominations have faced divisions and splits. Like the "house of Judah/David" in fifth-century Jerusalem, each group always finds solace and comfort in God and the Scriptures.

The question is, who is right? Both sides think they are, but the truth is that when a split occurs, *nobody* wins. The answer is found in the words of a carpenter from Nazareth who commanded that all people love God, their neighbor, and their enemies. As long as two sides are in dispute, God's will is being neglected.

What About Me?

• *When we are persecuted for our faith, God is near and does not forget us.* While it is rare to be persecuted for our faith in the United States, it does happen on occasion. However, it happens more often in other countries where religious freedom is neither allowed nor tolerated. On such occasions, apocalyptic literature encourages its readers to remain faithful to God even in the darkest of times.

• *In religious disputes, we are called to be faithful to God, not our ideas about God.* This is tough. Often we limit God to the size of our understanding instead of letting God expand our minds and hearts to take on the faith we need to be loyal servants. As noted in J. B. Phillips's *Your God Is Too Small*, we often have too small of a view of God. When disputes arise, we need to put aside our selfish interests and seek the true will of God.

• *Jesus is the best guide to help us through religious disputes.* For Christians, Jesus Christ is the only true vehicle for settling internal disputes. The familiar slogan "What would Jesus do?" is not just a recent marketing ploy for commercial publishers to make a lot of money; rather, the phrase's roots are in the New Testament. What *would* Jesus do? He would love, forgive, and heal. Why would we ever think it takes anything else?

Resources

Barbara Brown Taylor, Harry Vaughn Smith Lectures, Mercer University, "The Luminous Web: Addressing the Gap between Science and Religion" (24 March 1999) forthcoming as a book from Cowley.

Paul Hanson, *The Dawn of Apocalyptic: The Historical and Sociological Roots of Jewish Apocalyptic Eschatology* (Philadelphia: Fortress Press, 1975).

F. B. Huey, Jr., "Zechariah, Book of," *Mercer Dictionary of the Bible*, ed. Watson Mills (Macon: Mercer University Press, 1991) 981–2.

REASSURING THE FAITHFUL

Zechariah 12:1-10

Introduction

You may teach Bible studies for twenty years and never find a harder text to interpret than this one. One commentary on Zechariah 12 opens with this most "encouraging" statement: Zechariah 9–14 "contains some of the most obscure and difficult material in the entire corpus of Old Testament literature" (Robert C. Dentan, *The Interpreter's Bible*, vol. 6, New York: Abingdon Press, 1956, 1089). James T. Cleland, on the other hand, began his interpretation of Zechariah 12 by saying, "It is a 'pep talk' to the faithful and a nightmare to the sober interpreter" (Ibid., 1106).

Rather than wrestling with hard material like that found in Zechariah 12, most of us move on to parts of the Bible that are more easily understood. I admit that I've never tried to preach a sermon from this text, but to be sure, this material (Zech 9–14) held great significance for the writers of the New Testament. The Gospel writers especially depended on quoting Zechariah when they wrote of the suffering and death of Jesus, for the message is that out of great suffering, God can bring good. There was reason to hope. And that's the spirit of Zechariah 12. Things may be dark and it may appear that "bad people" are going to prevail, but God is still in charge, and God's people will not be destroyed. Remain faithful because God will find a way to save us and work out God's purposes.

The sense of all apocalyptic literature is similar to this: It looks as if things cannot get any worse. The only way to survive is for God to step in and save us. And God will do just that. So keep on believing, because just as God saved the Hebrews from Egypt and the Jews from Babylon, so God will save God's own today.

Because of the obscurity of our text, I will take a direct approach.

(1) The **Setting** will place the text in a historical context (though you must understand that commentators do not agree on which context is accurate).

(2) The **Story** will translate the text into language that we as contemporary learners can understand. (The present form is difficult indeed!)

(3) The **Meaning** will be sermonic, so saints can use this text to draw hope and help for the Church today.

The material for today is quite controversial, but the opinions I will offer are those most common among scholars. Just keep in mind that there is difference of opinion among people of both good *scholarship* and good *will*.

The Setting

Zechariah is an unusual book. The part actually recorded according to the ministry of Zechariah is found in chapters 1–8. Zechariah was a contemporary of Haggai, and his work spanned the years from 520 to 518 BC. He was very influential in the rebuilding of Jerusalem and the Temple. Judaism came of a small, devoted, intentional group. "Haggai was one of the founders of Judaism. So too was Zechariah" (D. Winton Thomas, "Zechariah," George Arthur Buttrick, ed., *The Interpreter's Bible*, vol. 6, New York: Abingdon Press, 1956, 1054). Zechariah was a person of great influence; however, chapters 9–14 (the second half of the book) were not written by Zechariah, nor do they describe life during Zechariah's time. In fact, "chapters 9–14, which nowhere claim to be from Zechariah, portray nothing of the early Persian period, but speak rather of the Greeks (see 9:13)" (*The New Oxford Annotated Bible*, New York: Oxford University Press, 1991, 1220 OT section).

Though this may sound strange to modern ears, it actually was common for unknown or less popular authors to attach their material to the work of someone more famous. We don't know who wrote our text. It was probably a disciple of Zechariah's teachings who wanted to borrow from his fame and influence. This opinion is shared nearly unanimously by all of Old Testament scholarship. But the question remains: who *did* write it? Quite simply, we don't know.

Do we at least know when was it written? Zechariah's public ministry lasted from 520 to 518 BC, soon after the Jews came back from Babylon to rebuild Jerusalem and the Temple. Persia was in control of the Middle East, and in fact, it was Persia's tolerance that allowed Judaism to rise from the ruins of captivity in Babylon. Obviously, the material in chapters 1–8 describes life in Jerusalem in 520 BC.

Our text for today, however, does not connect with Jerusalem in 520 BC. There is no date given, but the conditions described in Zechariah 9–14 clearly suggest that the Greeks have gained control (again, see 9:13). This would mean it was after 323 BC and the death of Alexander the Great. Neither Haggai, Zerubbabel, Ezra, Nehemiah, nor Zechariah are mentioned. We also find that shepherds are leaders. Clearly, we have no way to date the text. "Style, vocabulary, and theological ideas differentiate these chapters from Zechariah's work (chapters 1–8)" (*The New Oxford Annotated Bible*, 1220 OT section).

So, what we've established so far is that we don't know who wrote our text and we aren't certain when it was written. Right about now, you may be wondering, "Is there anything that we do know?" And the answer is yes.

(1) It was almost surely written during the time when the Greeks ruled the Jews (after 323 BC and before 165 BC). I suspect our text was written in either the fourth or third century BC.

(2) Clearly the Jews were being pressured to become Greek in religion as well as overall lifestyle. Many Jews resisted this pressure. It was a hard time, and for the faithful, a desperate time.

(3) Our text describes a confrontation: "All the nations of the earth shall come together against it (Jerusalem)" (Zech 12:3b NRSV). Would the faithful Jew survive? Would God intervene to save?

The Story

The language of apocalyptic literature is difficult by nature. For instance, a phrase or verse often can be interpreted in several ways—not to mention the fact that the descriptions sound as if they are from a science-fiction movie. My purpose in this section is to convert the ideas in the text into plain English.

(1) All of the nations attack, lay siege "against Jerusalem" (12:2-3), but the attack will not be successful. To "make Jerusalem a cup of reeling" (12:2a): As if they are drunk, those who attack Jerusalem will be unsteady on their feet. "Make Jerusalem a heavy stone for all the peoples" (12:3a): Stone-lifting contests were a prime pastime, and according to this text, as with one who tries to lift a stone that is too heavy, those who attack Jerusalem will only hurt themselves for their trouble.

(2) There is a battle between "all the nations" and the godly, who are both Jerusalem and Judah (see 12:3c). The heathen want to destroy the faithful, but God will not let this happen. "On that day, says the Lord, I will strike every horse with panic, and its rider with madness" (12:4). God intervened, and the heathen failed. God's people won the battle.

(3) There is tension between Jerusalem and Judah (the people of the city and the country)—the people of God. Instead of helping their city cousins, the people of Judah watched and waited. Then it became clear to them: God's people were in Jerusalem and they had an obligation to help. "The inhabitants of Judah shall say to themselves, 'The inhabitants of Jerusalem have strength through the Lord of hosts, their God'" (12:5b). When the people of Judah realized, "This is our fight," they hurried to join the people of Jerusalem.

(4) Judah fights with greater fury than do the people of Jerusalem. In fact, the greater share of glory goes to Judah: "The Lord will give victory to the tents of Judah first, that...the glory of the inhabitants of Jerusalem may not be exalted over that of Judah" (12:7).

(5) Even the weak people in Jerusalem will be protected and made strong (12:8). God will take care of God's people.

(6) God will punish any nations that fight against Jerusalem (12:9). There is a special relationship between the faithful Jew

and God. The covenant made at Sinai still holds. God not only loves the Jews, but also will fight for them, putting down the pagan, heathen, godless people who dare to wage war against them.

(7) Verse 10 has been applied to Jesus. Certainly there may have been a hero who died in battle, but all we really know is that someone died and all the faithful mourned.

The Meaning

If I were teaching this lesson in a classroom environment, here's the way I would apply it:

(1) Opposition to the serious Christian varies from both place to place and time to time, but this world is usually not very friendly to people who are serious about their faith.

In today's text, Greek culture was not just integrated into Judaism; it wanted to *replace* Judaism altogether. Those who resisted were under siege. I've met Christians who felt they were under siege. The text is speaking to us.

(2) Does God notice when we are surrounded, when "all the nations of the earth come together against" us? From both Old and New Testament alike, a picture of God emerges that is very broad:

• God is the creator of the world and of all people (12:1).
• God is the Lord of history; no matter how remote God may seem in the moment, God is in control.
• God preserves God's people. From Egypt, God extracted the Hebrews. From Babylon, God brought back a faithful remnant. From the cross, there emerged a faithful few. God always saves and preserves the people.
• God preserved the Jews and Christians because God cared about them. God is caring, loving, personal, and near. Any theology of God that is impersonal and uncaring is not in touch with the Bible.
• God cares for everyone. This idea goes beyond our text, but is fully developed in the New Testament. God's love reaches beyond the Jews to include Gentiles; Christians are both Jews and Gentiles. Christians are to reach out to everyone, because God cares for everyone.

W. T. Connor once taught theology at Southwestern Seminary. He was an old man when I got to the seminary, so I never had him as a professor. But he was invited to lecture to us one day. I wrote this line in the flyleaf of my textbook: "Intelligent men have stopped wondering if there is a god; now they are wondering what kind of god he is." I think that makes sense. The reason many people give no thought to God is because they have such a twisted picture of what God is like. They don't dismiss the God we know in Christ; rather, they dismiss the God who has been portrayed to them. It's hard to pray, "Our Father who art in heaven...," if the only way "father" has been defined for you has been absent or uncaring.

What is God like? Apocalyptic literature paints a picture of a God who fights for, cares for, and finally will come to save God's people. In those times when I feel like I'm the only Christian around and there is pressure to conform, I am going to remember this text. God has not forgotten me. Hang tough; God has not forgotten you either. Do the right thing. You are not alone. God will show up when needed.

Notes

Notes

2

THE BEASTS AND
THE HOLY ONES

Daniel 7:1-28

Central Question

How do you interpret God's promise of presence with us?

Scripture

Daniel 7:7-14 After this I saw in the visions by night a fourth beast, terrifying and dreadful and exceedingly strong. It had great iron teeth and was devouring, breaking in pieces, and stamping what was left with its feet. It was different from all the beasts that preceded it, and it had ten horns. 8 I was considering the horns, when another horn appeared, a little one coming up among them; to make room for it, three of the earlier horns were plucked up by the roots. There were eyes like human eyes in this horn, and a mouth speaking arrogantly. 9 As I watched, thrones were set in place, and an Ancient One took his throne, his clothing was white as snow, and the hair of his head like pure wool; his throne was fiery flames, and its wheels were burning fire. 10 A stream of fire issued and flowed out from his presence. A thousand thousands served him, and ten thousand times ten thousand stood attending him. The court sat in judgment, and the books were opened. 11 I watched then because of the noise of the arrogant words that the horn was speaking. And as I watched, the beast was put to death, and its body destroyed and given over to be burned with fire. 12 As for the rest of the beasts, their dominion was taken away, but their lives were prolonged for a season and a time. 13 As I watched in the night visions, I saw one like a human being coming with the clouds of heaven. And he came to the Ancient

One and was presented before him. 14 To him was given dominion and glory and kingship, that all peoples, nations, and
languages should serve him. His dominion is an everlasting
dominion that shall not pass away, and his kingship is one that
shall never be destroyed.

Remembering

Chapters 1–6 of Daniel compose a collection of stories set in the
time of the Babylonian Exile, and as one would assume, center on
the prophet by the same name. In chapters 1 and 3, Daniel and
his friends Shadrach, Meshach, and Abednego are faced with all
kinds of tests that examine their faithfulness to God. For
instance, in chapter 1 they are confronted with dietary laws that
threaten their obedience to the Law of Moses, and must prove
that a combination of diet and faith makes them stronger and
more productive.

Daniel interprets Nebuchadnezzar's dream from chapter 2—
after the king's court has failed to do so—and becomes a
top-ranked advisor. Then the three young Jewish men are challenged with the test of idolatry in chapter 3, and when they insist
on remaining loyal to God, they are thrown into the fiery furnace.
God delivers them to safety, however, and in turn, the Gentile
king worships the Jewish God. In chapter 4, Nebuchadnezzar
boasts of his own power, failing to recognize that true power
belongs to God. Although Nebuchadnezzar loses his mind for a
time, he eventually returns to his worship of God, and for that
reason, his sanity and kingdom are restored.

Chapters 5 and 6 are set with
different kings. In chapter 5, King
Belshazzar's arrogance leads to his
seeing the handwriting on the wall,
and in fact, his kingdom is over-
thrown that very night. Finally, in
chapter 6 is the story of Daniel and
the lions. Each of these stories is
concerned with how the Jews were
to live in exile. Even in the midst of

Nebuchadrezzar was
king of Babylonia for
43 years, from
605–562 BC (the name
has been standardized to
"Nebuchadnezzar" in most
English translations, but
"Nebuchadrezzar" is the form
truest to the original) (Crawford,
607). In Daniel, the NRSV uses
the "Nebuchadnezzar" spelling.

persecution and life in a foreign society, they were to be faithful to the commandments of God and face life with courage.

In chapters 7–12, the literary style of the book switches from narratives to the recounting of visions. In fact, it is in Daniel 7–12 where we find the first fully developed apocalyptic material (see unit introduction). While chapters 1–6 were set during the Babylonian Exile, they were not collected and shaped into their completed form until around the second century. Likewise, chapters 7–12 were written and compiled between 167–164 BC. The Jews in and around Jerusalem had fallen under control of the Greeks, specifically Antiochus Epiphanes IV, who had placed a statue of Zeus in the Temple in Jerusalem. The response of one family—the Maccabees—led to a revolution, which resulted in the miraculous defeat of Antiochus by the small, ill-equipped Jewish force, an event still celebrated today known as Hanukkah.

Studying

(7:1-8) As is typical of apocalyptic literature, Daniel's vision is set in the past to show how it has come true at the present moment (see unit introduction). No longer is he just the interpreter, but now Daniel is the dreamer as well. Verses 2-8 vividly describe his dream: Four winds of heaven blow on the sea, and out of the sea come four beasts, representing four successive kingdoms. The use of animals and figures in the vision served as a way of coding the message for its audience, so the enemy would have no way of knowing who or what was being represented through its images. Nevertheless, the Jews knew.

Daniel's vision is set in the sixth century. It is interesting to note that Belshazzar was never the king of Babylon, but was only the regent while King Nabonidas was away (v. 1). Belshazzar is used here because he is present in chapter 5.

The first beast was a lion with the wings of an eagle, which were plucked off. The beast was made to stand on the ground like a human. Then a human mind was given to it. This beast signified the kingdom of Babylon, and the king was Nebuchadnezzar (see 4:36).

The second beast was a bear raised on its side with three tusks in its mouth. Having been told to devour many bodies, this creature represented the Median Empire (see 5:28). Incidentally, although the Median attack had been predicted (Jer 51:11), it never actually occurred. The Medes were a tyrannical power nonetheless, infamous for their savagery.

The third beast, denoting the Persian Empire, resembled a leopard and had four wings and four heads (see Dan 5:28). The wings may have been intended to symbolize how quickly this empire had risen under Cyrus (see Isa 41:2-3; 45:1).

The fourth beast was "terrifying and dreadful and exceedingly strong." With iron teeth and crushing, stomping feet, it was quite different from the other beasts. With ten horns—and one little horn emerging from those—this animal was indicative of the kingdom of the Greeks under the leadership of Alexander the Great (334–23 BC). The ten horns represented the ten divisions of the Greek kingdom, and the little horn—which, according to the text, spoke "arrogantly"—is identified as Antiochus Epiphanes IV. You will remember that Antiochus was the one who performed the "desolating sacrilege" (see Dan 8:13-14) by placing a statue of Zeus in the Jerusalem temple and offering swine as sacrifices on the Jewish altar.

> Nebuchadnezzar loses his sanity, but when he returns to the worship of God, his sanity is restored. Nebuchadnezzar says, "At that time my reason returned to me; and my majesty and splendor were restored to me for the glory of my kingdom. My counselors and my lords sought me out. I was re-established over my kingdom, and still more greatness was added to me" (Dan 4:36).

Other sources record that during this time in history, anyone in Israel found with the Law of Moses or who kept the Law of Moses was put to death. Any mother who had their sons circumcised was put to death, and the infant was killed as well. This was the context surrounding the book of Daniel. No wonder the people needed a message of hope to get them through their daily lives of persecution and the constant threat of death!

(7:9-14) The scene now changes to Daniel's seeing God on God's throne (v. 9-10). While there, in the midst of the heavenly residents, the "books were opened." "Books" are a common element of apocalyptic literature, and any reference to them suggests that secrets are about to be revealed.

The "arrogant" words of the little horn led to his (Antiochus's) death and to his body's (the Greek kingdom) being destroyed. Exactly how this was done is not disclosed at this point, but verses 13-14 provide a clue. To the throne room came "one like a human being." Because this phrase is usually translated, "like a son of man," it is often misinterpreted as implying Jesus Christ. Nothing, however, could be further from the original intent of the author of this text. This is essentially a "fifth Kingdom" and is initiated by God through God's servant, "one like a human being." There is a great deal of speculation over the identity of this individual. Although some have identified it with the Messiah, as mentioned, neither the words "messiah" nor "Davidic ruler"—nor anything close to those terms—are ever used. Elsewhere in Daniel, however, this description is used of angelic figures (8:15; 9:21; 10:16,18). The most likely figure the phrase refers to is Michael, the archangel who is described as the protector of Israel (see Dan 10:13-14, 20-21; 12:1). Led by the victory of Michael and governed by God, the "fifth" Kingdom would never fall, as did the four kingdoms just described.

(7:15-28) In this section Daniel asks for and receives a divine interpretation of his dream from "one of the attendants." After the four kingdoms pass, the fifth will be given to the "holy ones of the Most High" (v. 18). The King James Version reads, "the saints of the most High." In the 17th century, the Puritans thought this to be a direct reference to them, and in fact they were not the last group to believe such. Many "Christian" groups have believed (and some still do) that they are God's "holy ones," and that they are the sole heirs to the eternal Kingdom. The "holy ones" are those who remain faithful to God in all circumstances. Whether in times of plenty or in times of crisis, those who are faithful to God are the heirs to the fifth Kingdom.

In verses 19-22 Daniel desires to know the truth regarding the fourth beast and the "little horn" that makes war with the "holy ones." In verses 23-27 the truth comes out in typical apocalyptic fashion: The kingdom of Alexander the Great did not conquer the entire earth, but Alexander and his generals (ten of them, but there is wide disagreement as to which ten) did march through a large portion of it, namely from Macedonia to the near and far east (v. 23). It was the emergence of the "little horn" that concerned the writer most (v. 24-27). Antiochus Ephiphanes IV did have control for a time, but the Maccabean revolt was successful with God's direction. The result was that Jerusalem (the kingdom) was given back to the "holy ones."

> The Maccabees were the Jewish leaders who spearheaded the revolution in 167 BC that resulted in the formation of an independent Jewish state in Judea that endured until 63 BC, when it fell under Roman domination (Songer, 533).

Verse 28 notes that Daniel kept the matter in his mind. Again, in typical apocalyptic literary fashion, the secrets are "kept" until the end. In this case, the end was at the time of the victory over Antiochus Epiphanes IV.

Understanding

The obvious question is, if all the events in Daniel 7 have already occurred, then what does this text mean today? This is a valid question. Many people believe this text is about the end of the world. But it's not. Like all apocalyptic literature, the book of Daniel was written to give hope and encouragement to those in situations of crisis and persecution. However, that these events have already happened does not diminish their importance for today. Indeed, it is important to know that these events described in Daniel 7 did occur and that the true servants of God remained faithful. Some lost their lives by believing in God, while others led a revolution. Whether one believes that these events are still imminent or in the past, the truth of the matter is that God, who is always faithful, demands *our* faithfulness as well. It is to the faithful, "the holy ones," that the fifth, eternal Kingdom belongs.

But what exactly does being faithful even during such difficult times entail? After all, our "persecutions" are different than they were 2,200 years ago. Our "enemies"—to use the term in the book of Psalms—are often ill health, the loss of loved ones, or financial ruin due to bad investments or loss of jobs. Despite all of these potential "persecutions," we are encouraged by the book of Daniel to stay strong in our faith. How can we do this? Prayer or communication with God is a good start. Daniel and his friends were constantly praying to God. But sometimes even this is not enough.

God never promises to deliver us from our enemies, although we pray for it everyday (see Ps 23). What God does promise throughout the entire Bible is to be with us. We are never alone. Our faithfulness is not in deliverance, but in presence—God's presence.

Have you ever noticed what makes a great Christmas? You can have a huge tree, lights, decorations, presents, food, and music, but if you have no one to share them with, it seems less like Christmas. Christmas is about presence, both God's presence and human presence. At Christmastime, being with people who love each other beats all of the material presents in the world. There might be only one person with you or even twenty, but presence is better than being alone. God never leaves us alone. God is present—with us (*Emmanuel*) even to the end of the world.

What About Me?

• *Does Daniel 7 have a word of hope and encouragement for me?*
Regardless of our situation, Daniel 7 tells us that no human-constructed form of government or environment will stand the test of time. Only if God is in control do we have the opportunity

to live life to its fullest. What assures you that God is in control? How does the belief that God is in control alter your perspective on the difficulties of the present?

• *We can learn much about God from history.* While many people may not appreciate such a history lesson as you have read today, it is critical to know that God works in history. The patterns of God's work in the past are the best indicators as to how God will work in the present and in the future. How do stories such as this one from Daniel encourage your understanding of God's presence with us? How do you rely on the biblical story to encourage your faith? Which biblical story or stories provide you with insight as to how God is working in your life?

• *God promises to be present with us.* God does not promise to deliver us from difficulty, hardship, or pain, but God always offers presence. We never have to face anything alone.

Resources

John J. Collins, *Daniel*, Hermeneia (Minneapolis: Fortress Press, 1993).

Timothy G. Crawford, "Nebuchadrezzar," *Mercer Dictionary of the Bible*, ed. Watson E. Mills et al. (Macon GA: Mercer University Press, 1990) 607.

Mitchell G. Reddish, "Daniel," *Mercer Commentary on the Bible*, vol. 4 (Macon GA: Mercer University Press, 1996) 217–34.

THE BEASTS AND THE HOLY ONES

Daniel 7:1-28

Introduction

Apocalyptic literature is not for Sunday afternoon pleasure reading. Many people will be unfamiliar with it and intimidated by it. I am not as sure of myself when trying to interpret what the text means, so therefore, I am a bit uneasy when preaching from it. And I do not think I am alone. Most pastors tread softly when dealing with apocalyptic literature. Now, if this is the way most pastors feel about teaching and preaching from the apocalyptic, how must lay people feel?

Having confessed discomfort with this part of the Bible, let's go forward. If we talk about all the people who dwell on Revelation and those who keep predicting the end of time from Daniel, we never will get to the actual lesson. Our job is to bring our minds to these texts, to try to determine what they meant to the people who first read them, and finally, to establish what they mean for us. Nothing in the Bible is useless or without present application. Granted, some parts of the Bible are easier to interpret than others, and this can make things difficult, but not impossible.

Apocalyptic Literature

(1) "Apocalyptic" implies disclosure, unveiling, or revelation.
(2) Apocalyptic literature is relayed through two mediums:
• Visions—"Daniel had a dream and visions of his head as he lay in bed" (Dan 7:1 NRSV).
• Journeys—The writer is taken into another world and the mysteries of our life are "explained."

• Both visions and journeys had an interpreter, typically an angel.

(3) There are several marks of apocalyptic literature:
• Symbolic visions are often fantastic, surreal.
• Numbers are given veiled significance, as in the case of "666."
• Secret books are locked. Someday they will be opened.
• Often apocalyptic literature is eschatological, involving predictions about what is going to happen in the future.
• Dualism is frequent. The "present age" is bad, but the "Age to Come"—a new creation—will be better.

(4) Uniformly, apocalyptic literature springs from persecution and hard times. This world is bad, hard, and mean, but our hope lies in another life. Don't give up, because God will come.

(5) These authors' beliefs about God are basic to the way they interpreted history. They deeply believed that God was in control of history, that God knew the predicament of those who were suffering. And in good time, God would move to rescue them. Further, they believed the only hope for relief was in God.

(6) Concluding thoughts about apocalyptic literature:
• It has had a strong, enduring appeal. The appetite for an "explanation" of the books of Revelation and Daniel continues. The preacher who claims to know what they mean will have an audience.
• It has sustained God's people through hard times. From Black slaves in the 19th century to suffering saints in Communist countries, all have found hope in biblical apocalyptic passages.

The Book of Daniel

Here are some details to help you find your way through the book of Daniel. Not all of them will be "traditional."

(1) Daniel is composed of six stories (chps. 1–6) and four visions (chps. 7–12). Set in the sixth century BC, the six stories are about Daniel and his life in Babylon. The second part, however, is different. The four visions are set "in the Seleucid/Ptolemaic

struggle over Palestine in the second century BC" (John Joseph Owens, *Broadman Commentary*, vol. 6, Nashville: Broadman Press, 1971, 375).

(2) The contrasts between the two sections of the book are stark:

- The first six chapters are clear; the last six are obscure.
- The first six chapters speak of Daniel in the third person; the last six employ Daniel's viewpoint.
- The first six are biography; the last six are autobiography.
- The first six chapters are set in the Babylonian-Persian era, and the last six chapters come from the second century BC.

(3) Today's text (Dan 7) comes from the second half of the book, which is taken from a second-century BC setting. Unless we know what was going on with the godly Jews in that time, we will miss the message. What historical events prompted this writing?

- Babylon took Jewish leaders captive in 587 BC. That captivity lasted 70 years, during which Babylon was defeated and made subject to Persia. Under Persia, godly Jews were allowed to return to Jerusalem and re-establish both city and Temple worship.
- In due time, Persia would fall to the Greeks and Alexander the Great (334 BC). The introduction of Greek culture into Jewish life had profound influence.

(4) Now we've come to the text. Alexander is dead, and the Greek kingdom has been divided into four parts. The Palestine/Jewish part has fallen to the Seleucid family. Through veiled language, we are introduced to a member of this family, Antiochus IV, who ruled the Jews from 175 to 164 BC. This man, whose name means "Antiochus the Manifest" or "Antiochus who is God," publicly called himself God. He was the youngest son in his family; another should have ruled, but Antiochus pushed him aside (see 7:8). "He is known as one of the cruelest tyrants of all time, enterprising like his father, yet furious and precipitate almost to the degree of madness. His relations with Jerusalem and the Jews were particularly unfortunate" (*The Interpreter's Dictionary of the Bible*, New York: Abingdon Press, 1962, 150).

- He was arrogant and acted as if he were a god.

• He was intent on making Greeks of Jews. All things Greek were good; all things Jewish, on the other hand, were bad. Sometimes you will hear this philosophy described as "Hellenization."
• In 168 BC, he decided Jerusalem should be wiped out, so he colonized with Greeks. An army he sent entered Jerusalem on a Sabbath, killed most of the males, and made slaves of the women and children. Those men who escaped joined Judas Maccabeus in resistance.
• Antiochus issued a decree that there should be one religion, one universal law. Jews who resisted were killed.

A pagan altar dedicated to Zeus was built to replace the altar in the Temple devoted to Yahweh God. Jews were ordered to take part in pagan worship; if they did not, they were killed. It was during this time that the second part of Daniel was written. People were under extreme persecution. To remain faithful to the God of Abraham and Moses was a great risk, but to deny God was to ignore conscience.

In this peril, a writer told of Daniel, one who survived in Babylon. Daniel was told to stop serving his God, but he refused. He was persecuted, but God saved him from the lion's den. Daniel was the model for Jews during the madness of Antiochus IV.

The Meaning of Our Text

These Scriptures are difficult to understand, and much material is published that seeks to explain who the beasts were and what it all means. There is quite a difference in opinion over how to label parts of this vision. However, there is unity surrounding the basic meaning of our text.

(1) "The great sea" (7:2) refers to the chaos that surrounded the Jews as these words were written.

(2) "Four great beasts" (7:3a) came out of the chaos. There is a great difference of opinion concerning how to identify them. Here is mine:
• The winged lion represents Babylon.
• The bear signifies the Medes.

• The leopard is suggestive of the Persians.

• The awful fourth creature symbolizes the Greeks.

(3) The emphasis in our text is on the fourth creature. The first three beasts are introduced and quickly dismissed.

(4) The "ten horns" (7:7c) are the Greeks who followed Alexander the Great to the throne.

(5) Another horn appears, "a little one coming up among them" (7:8b). This is Antiochus Epiphanes, the real tormentor of the Jews.

(6) The "vision" is given in 7:2-14, succeeded by the request for help understanding 7:15-18. Interpretation comes in 7:19-28.

(7) The "Ancient One" who comes to sit in judgment is God. Throne, "clothing white as snow," hair like "pure wool"—these all define the goodness and purity of God.

(8) "One like a human being" (7:13) is a symbol of the faithful Jews, the ones who have proven themselves in great persecution.

So, how does it turn out?

(1) God takes note of the suffering people. Already, a court is set up to judge the cruelty and blasphemy of "the little horn." "This horn made war with the holy ones and was prevailing over them until the Ancient One came" (7:21). Truly this was the condition of the Jews for several years while Antiochus Epiphanes battered them.

(2) "He (the little horn) shall speak words against the Most High, shall wear out the holy ones of the Most High, and shall attempt to change the sacred seasons and the law" (7:25a). Antiochus Epiphanes tried to do away with Jewish worship and replace it with Greek worship.

(3) God will put up with folly and vanity for a season, but it will not last long. God has appointed a time for Antiochus Epiphanes's defeat. "They (the faithful Jews) shall be given into his power for a time, two times, and a half a time" (7:25b). Owens notes that the three and a half years that Daniel covers almost exactly make up the period of suffering. The agony began in June 168 BC and ended "with the rededication of the Temple, December 165 (1 Macc 4:52; ca. three and one half years)" (*The Broadman Commentary*, 428).

(4) Evil was punished, and good rewarded. "Then the court shall sit in judgment, and his dominion shall be taken away, to be consumed and totally destroyed" (7:26). Antiochus's rule did not last. "The kingship...shall be given to the people of the Most High; their kingdom shall be an everlasting kingdom..." (7:27). The faithful Jews would receive an everlasting Kingdom as well as the blessing of God.

What does all this mean to us?

(1) God notices the pain of God's people, and especially those who "suffer for righteousness."

(2) History belongs to God, who is completely in control. When a "Hitler" or some other brute appears overpowering, it is only what seems to be. I remember how amazed I was at the way the Iron Curtain came down as if by the hand of God. Once again, tyrants were passing and God affirmed that suffering is not forever.

(3) God gives a place to God's own. Though injustice and suffering have their seasons, the faithful will inherit the earth in God's time. Faithfulness to God is noticed and rewarded.

We live in good times. Most of us have more than enough to eat, freedom and blessings beyond what most people who have lived on this planet could imagine. Wickedness, however, is still with us. Wide-scale brutality is not just in history books. Kosovo is an illustration still fresh on our minds. But when the world seems crazy and out-of-control, remember this text. Though it is cast in a language foreign to us, the message is one of comfort and hope.

Notes

Notes

3

FRETTING OVER
THE FUTURE

Daniel 7:1-28

Central Question

How do you face the future?

Scripture

Daniel 12:1-13 "At that time Michael, the great prince, the protector of your people, shall arise. There shall be a time of anguish, such as has never occurred since nations first came into existence. But at that time your people shall be delivered, everyone who is found written in the book. 2 Many of those who sleep in the dust of the earth shall awake, some to everlasting life, and some to shame and everlasting contempt. 3 Those who are wise shall shine like the brightness of the sky, and those who lead many to righteousness, like the stars forever and ever. 4 But you, Daniel, keep the words secret and the book sealed until the time of the end. Many shall be running back and forth, and evil shall increase." 5 Then I, Daniel, looked, and two others appeared, one standing on this bank of the stream and one on the other. 6 One of them said to the man clothed in linen, who was upstream, "How long shall it be until the end of these wonders?" 7 The man clothed in linen, who was upstream, raised his right hand and his left hand toward heaven. And I heard him swear by the one who lives forever that it would be for a time, two times, and half a time, and that when the shattering of the power of the holy people comes to an end, all these things would be accomplished. 8 I heard but could not understand; so I said, "My lord, what shall be the outcome of these things?" 9 He said, "Go your way, Daniel, for the words are to remain secret and sealed until the time of the end. 10 Many shall be purified, cleansed, and refined, but the wicked shall continue to act wickedly. None of the wicked shall understand, but those who are wise shall understand. 11 From the time that the regular burnt offering is taken away and the abomination that desolates is set up, there shall be one thousand two hundred ninety days. 12 Happy are those who persevere and attain the thousand three hundred thirty-five days. 13 But you, go your way, and rest; you shall rise for your reward at the end of the days."

Remembering

The book of Daniel is the only example of apocalyptic literature in the Old Testament. In last week's session, we studied Daniel 7 in the context of the second century, when the Jews in Jerusalem encountered the evil reign of Antiochus Epiphanes IV. The author of Daniel uses coded language and secretive agendas to communicate the message of hope to those facing persecution. In fact, chapters 8 and 9 in particular are two of the most encoded texts in the Bible. For instance, the "male-goat" in Daniel 8 actually represents Alexander the Great, and the "great horn between its eyes" signifies Antiochus (8:20-22). The angel Gabriel (see Lk 1:26) interprets the vision for Daniel, instructing him to "seal up the vision" until the time comes for it to be read and understood.

"The book of Daniel was written for a very specific situation in the Maccabean era, but retained its significance long after that era had passed.... Daniel also had a more general influence in shaping the apocalyptic expectations of early Christianity that found their most vivid expression in the Revelation of John" (Collins, 197).

Daniel 9 is dominated initially by Daniel's righteous prayer, before moving to a reinterpretation of Jeremiah's prophecy of a 70-year Exile (the Babylonian Exile). Daniel reinterprets the "70" to mean 70 weeks of years—that is, 490 years. But the writer is not as concerned with the first 69 weeks as with the last week. The "anointed one" in 9:26 refers to Onias III, the high priest in Jerusalem who was removed from office in 175 BC and murdered

in 171 BC. In 9:27, the "little horn" (or Antiochus Epiphanes IV) offers "an abomination that desolates," and at the end of three and a half years, war will break out against him. Although some have thought this to be in reference to the anti-Christ, it is actually about Antiochus, who set up a statue of Zeus in the Temple and offered burnt offerings on the altar of God, an act of blatant blasphemy.

The phrase "abomination of desolation" in Daniel and the synoptic Gospels refers to something disgusting which pollutes the worship of God. In Daniel 12:11 reference is to the detestable profanation of the Jerusalem Temple by Antiochus IV, who set up an altar upon which sacrifices were offered to the Olympian Zeus. The altar to Zeus may have included an image of Zeus bearing the features of Antiochus IV, who was surnamed Epiphanes ("the manifest [God]"), thus deepening the repugnance (Mauldin, 5).

Chapters 10–12 compose a lengthy section about the conflict of the nations with the heavenly powers. It is in essence a history from the time of the Persian Empire through the author's era, the second century. Its culmination results in the rise of Antiochus Epiphanes IV to power. Using coded language from the time of the real Daniel in the sixth century down to the time of the actual writing of the book, the writer has produced a history written in a very skilled apocalyptic style. Putting words into the mouth of a real prophet from the past enables the writer to communicate to the reader that everything that has happened has been foretold. During the second century BC, worship was interrupted, the Law was prohibited from being read, and new religions were overwhelming the temple. Only God could change this. In the meantime, the question each believer had to answer was, "How do I face the future?" Is your faith strong enough to keep you believing—even when all seems lost?

Studying

The Resurrection (12:1-4) "Michael" is the "one like a human being" (7:28), the one intended to lead the cosmic forces over the evil enemy. This kind of cosmic battle in which the forces of good win over the forces of evil—usually behind a great warrior—is a common theme in apocalyptic literature. Already familiar to the reader (Dan 10:13-14, 20-21), Michael is such a figure here. The "time of anguish" was a reference to Antiochus Epiphanes IV's reign over Judea. Although many have tried to associate this terrible time with the period of tribulation invented by end-of-the-world doomsayers, it certainly was *not* the end of the world.

> The archangel Michael is sometimes referred to as the "patron" or "guardian angel" of Israel. According to Daniel 12:1, he will be instrumental in the final deliverance of God's people (Gloer, 575).

As you discuss this lesson in your Bible study room, imagine that an opposing army from a distant country interrupts you and closes the church doors. Next, they tell you that if you are caught reading from the Bible again, you will be imprisoned and executed. It seems unthinkable, doesn't it? But that is essentially what happened to the Jews in Judea when Antiochus Epiphanes IV set up his control in their country. In fact, the book of Daniel was written for a people such as that. It was a time of anguish. Deliverance, however, awaits those who persevere and are "written in the book" (see Ex 32:32-33; Ps 69:28; Isa 4:3).

But what of those who are faithful, yet die anyway? The answer is in verse 2: they "shall awake...to everlasting life." While reward and long life are promises commonly made to the faithful in the Old Testament, resurrection is not. In fact, this is the only undisputed text regarding individual resurrection in the Old Testament. Many texts, however, mention the restoration of the nation of Israel (for example, Ezek 37), but only here is it characterized as a reward to an individual believer.

The same is true of those who will "awake...to shame and everlasting contempt." Elsewhere in the Old Testament, the evil who die simply go to the grave—or Sheol—but here the writer understands for the first time in Israel's history that the faithful are to be resurrected to life with God and the unfaithful to shame. Daniel is instructed in verse 4 to keep the words secret until the end. The book is set in Babylon in the sixth century, but the "end" is at the time of the writer in the second century. So, the words no longer need to be kept secret, but should be read and proclaimed in the streets.

Final Advice (12:5-12) "Two others" like Gabriel stand with Daniel, offering him final advice and answers. The length of time for this "anguish" is again coded, but the original readers knew it was nearly over. Unfortunately, as verse 10 makes clear, one of the angels tells Daniel (and us) that many will be faithful, "but the wicked shall continue to act wickedly." With the death of Antiochus Epiphanes IV and the removal of Zeus from the temple, each generation from that day on would have to face their own "Antiochus Epiphanes IV," their own anguish. The text remains cloaked or coded enough that each faith community can interpret this book to their own benefit, to encourage them when times are tough and persecution is knocking on the door.

Verses 11-12 are two different calculations in attempts to answer the question of how long persecution would go on. While the dates are no longer valid, the message is the same: persecution and anguish are not over in a day, but will more than likely take more time than preferred.

Receive Your Reward (12:13) The last verse of this apocalyptic book promises that Daniel "shall rise for [his] reward at the end of days." In chapter one of the book of Daniel, the character Daniel is portrayed as the model believer—first as faithful to the Law of Moses, a loyal friend and interpreter, and now as loyal messenger. Let the reader understand: to live your life as Daniel did is to have the promise of resurrection.

Understanding

Much like the Albanians who were thrown out of their houses and cities, the Jews of the second century faced their own "Slobodan Milosevic." It seems that every generation has a different name for the same oppressor. Earlier this century, there was Hitler and Stalin, before that it was the Inquisition, and so on. Today many Christians are persecuted for their faith in many third world countries. Amazingly enough, the church has been as guilty of persecuting believers as have the states and countries.

Many persecuted people find comfort in the book of Daniel. Comfort comes not at the close of persecution, but in knowing that you are faithful to God and that you can look forward to the promised resurrection.

When a loved one has died, however, the last thing we want to hear is, "It should make you happy to know that they're with Jesus, and one day you'll be reunited." True, but hardly the thing to say to one who is grieving. What the grieving person wants is to have their loved one back, not a promise of seeing them in the future. It is very important, then, to know that resurrection awaits us after death. This is the crux of Christianity. There is more to this life than just "this life." There is life with God. Peter Kreeft notes that we all suffer from an incurable disease: death. The words of Daniel serve to remind us that there is not more *to* this life, but rather, there is more *than* this life. In this life, people suffer and die. Even God's own Son demonstrated this, but he also demonstrated what is our only hope: resurrection. Christians can look forward to this prospect with an open heart. Apocalyptic literature helps us anticipate the day when there will be no illness, no sorrow, and no death—when life will be restored. Life "happens" with God, whether it is in the present or in the future.

What About Me?

• *Am I being persecuted?* If you are reading this material, then chances are that you are not. If you live in the United States, fortunately your faith is *your* business. So find out who is being persecuted for their faith, and when you find out, do something about it. Anything.

• *The book of Daniel is about the future, but not about the end of time.* Many look to Daniel to figure out when Christ will return (for the answer, jump ahead to next week's session), but this book is not about that kind of humanly-configured future. Rather, it is about the future of each individual who follows God. There is no need to fear the future, for the future is resurrection.

• *Faith is never easy.* Jesus said that our faith needs to be only the size of a mustard seed. That's not much. Seeing others who have endured much and are still faithful helps us to strengthen our own faith as well. Whom do you know that is a model of faith? Daniel was such a person. The challenge for us is to be like Daniel.

Resources

John J. Collins, *Daniel*, Hermeneia (Minneapolis: Fortress Press, 1993).

John J. Collins, "Daniel," *Mercer Dictionary of the Bible*, ed. Watson E. Mills et al. (Macon GA: Mercer University Press, 1990).

Hulitt Gloer, "Michael," *Mercer Dictionary of the Bible*, ed. Watson E. Mills et al. (Macon GA: Mercer University Press, 1990).

Frank Mauldin, "Abomination of Desolation," *Mercer Dictionary of the Bible*, ed. Watson E. Mills et al. (Macon GA: Mercer University Press, 1990).

Mitchell G. Reddish, "Daniel," *Mercer Commentary on the Bible*, vol. 4 (Macon: Mercer University Press, 1996) 217–34.

FRETTING OVER THE FUTURE

Daniel 7:1-28

Introduction

All of the general information about Greeks, Antiochus IV, Hellenization, and suffering discussed in last week's session still is useful in today's session. Daniel receives a vision telling him how much longer the brutal persecution of the faithful will last. The vision lifts the veil, and Daniel is given a peek into the future. Finally, he knows how long God will tolerate the abuse of the people. Relief will come and the pain will end, but not for three and a half years. But that's all God is willing to reveal. Obviously, the faithful need to hold on and not give up.

The most interesting part of Daniel 12 is exactly what our title highlights. After the prophet was given the answer to the question on the mind of every suffering Jew ("When will this misery and abuse end?"), he pushed a little further: "I heard but could not understand; so I said, 'My lord, what shall be the outcome of these things'" (Dan 12:8 NRSV)? Daniel wanted to know what would happen to the Jews after Antiochus was gone. He had tasted a vision of the future and now he wanted more. "Fretting over the Future" precisely captures the essence of our text. Last week we had to dig deep into ancient history. This week we plumb human nature.

The Bible is chock full of passages that tell of people's pushing God to tell them what the future holds.

Moses was as close to God as anyone in the Old Testament, and that closeness encouraged Moses' desire to see more of God. "Show me your glory, I pray" (Ex 33:18a). God granted part of Moses' request. He was allowed to look on "my back; but my face shall not be seen" (Ex 33:23b).

• Throughout the Gospels, the disciples push Jesus to tell them when things will happen, when the end will come. Their closeness to Jesus gave them a glimpse of God's future, and they wanted to know more.

When I drive cross-country, I often listen to the radio. Sometimes I tune in to a preacher. As often as not, the preacher is turning and twisting a text about the future. People want to know about the future—just like Daniel did—so they push preachers to search the Scriptures for a clue as to what God has in store for us. The reason some preachers are able to make a living fumbling around in prophecy is the near insatiable hunger people have to know what lies ahead. From Moses to Daniel to present-day disciples, we all want to know what God has in store.

"Go your way, Daniel, for the words are to remain secret and sealed until the time of the end" (12:9a). In other words, "I'm not going to tell you any more." For many, that leaves too much unsaid. While God did not tell Daniel what would happen to the Jews after the persecution of Antiochus IV, this text tells us a lot about God.

"Anguish" Happens, 12:1.

"There shall be a time of anguish such as has never occurred since nations first came into existence" (12:1b). "A time of anguish" appears throughout the Bible in a seemingly regular pattern.

The children of Israel were in slavery in Egypt. "Out of the slavery their cry for help rose up to God. God heard their groaning..." (Ex 2:23b-24a). It was a time of anguish, but it didn't last forever. God heard their cry and delivered them.

The ancient Hebrews offended God, and God allowed Babylon to attack Jerusalem and destroy the Temple. The people were killed, scattered, and taken captive. From Babylon, Ezekiel cried out to God for relief, and in chapter 37, he has a vision of "dry bones." God had not forgotten the people. What was dead would live again.

Toward the end of the New Testament, the people of God are being abused and persecuted by Rome. These suffering Christians cry out to God. James steadies the Church, saying,

"My brothers and sisters, whenever you face trials of any kind, consider it nothing but joy, because you know that the testing of your faith produces endurance..." (Jas 1:2-3a). And though the testing made them strong, it was a time of anguish. In due time, God heard the cries of the saints and offered relief.

We would prefer a world without anguish, but unfortunately, it likely will never happen. God's people share this planet with folks who know nothing of God's ways. In theory, the Church is supposed to be an ideal, but there is pain even in the Church. In fact, some people have experienced their deepest anguish in church work. Sadly, Church is not heaven on earth; rather, Church is a "halfway house on the road to heaven." That doesn't mean that we don't have a responsibility to work to make this world a better place, but in order to be rid of the anguish, we will have to go to another.

Michael Comes, 12:1a.

Michael was the patron angel of the Jews (see 10:12-14), God's agent to deliver. Chapter 12 begins, "At that time Michael, the great prince, the protector of your people, shall arise" (12:1a). The text says that Michael will rise, which means that God will act.

The Jews were convinced that deliverance could come only from God. This dependence on God is hard for contemporary Americans to understand. We have solved riddles in science, bringing parts of nature under our control. We can predict everything from hurricanes to tornadoes. We've whipped gravity; we can fly. We can communicate with each other from across the world. Why call on God for deliverance when we can solve our problems on our own?

Human beings have done some remarkable things. Science has served us well and promises to serve us better yet. For instance, the well-intentioned efforts of the world are combined to bring peace and sanity, prosperity and community, to Kosovo. But that will not remove the memory, the hate, or the intent of revenge. These enduring, persistent sicknesses are of the soul. Our children's children will be able to do many things we cannot, but unless God's angel comes to purge us of the anger, meanness, and memory that make us hateful, we will be none the better for anything science can do. A secular society urges, "Forget Michael; we don't need him anymore. Angels are for ancients, primitives." But not so fast! We need all the angels God is willing to send— then *and* now.

Resurrection, 12:2.

"But at that time your people shall be delivered, everyone who is found written in the book. Many of those who sleep in the dust of the earth shall awake, some to everlasting life, and some to shame..." (12:1b-2). "This is the first clear reference to resurrection in the Bible" (Notes from *The New Oxford Annotated Bible*, New York: Oxford University Press, 1991, 1147, OT section).

It is amazing that the great ones in the Old Testament lived and died without hope of resurrection. Late in the Old Testament, however, resurrection becomes a possibility. Job contains a reference that teases us, when out of his suffering, he declares,

O that my words were written down!
O that they were inscribed in a book!
O that with an iron pen and with lead
they were engraved on a rock forever!
For I know that my Redeemer lives,
and that at the last he will stand upon the earth;
and after my skin has been thus destroyed,
then in my flesh I shall see God,
whom I shall see on my side, not another. (Job 19:23-27)

Daniel takes resurrection from the obscure to the obvious. What is implied in Job is firmly stated in Daniel. The possibility of "everlasting life" appears in the text (12:2b). We must wait until the New Testament for Jesus to flesh out our doctrine of resurrection, but it all begins in Daniel.

The part of the text that leaves us dangling is the section about our being raised from death: "Many of those who sleep in the dust of the earth shall awake" (12:2a). I wonder why "many...who sleep" does not read instead, "all who sleep," but I have no good answer to this question.

I suspect the real question that bothered Daniel was this: Some Jews had risked, and many had sacrificed, their lives in faithfulness to God. These believers deserve a reward. However, others "cut a deal" with the Greeks, saving their skin at the price of their conscience. Daniel wonders if God will take note. Will the faithful be rewarded? The answer seems to be yes. And what of the accommodators, the clever people who saved themselves? The text suggests that God will take note of them, too. Both reward and punishment are implied.

In Hebrews, we find a parallel theme. The author of Hebrews discusses the fate of those who saved themselves at the price of denying Christ. "For it is impossible to restore again to repentance those who have once been enlightened, ...and have fallen away, since on their own they are crucifying again the Son of God and are holding him up to contempt" (Heb 6:4-6). The possibility of falling from grace is a theme most of us avoid, but Daniel and the author of Hebrews want to know if God is watching. Will faithfulness be rewarded? Will denying one's faith be punished? Neither Daniel nor the Hebrews give all the answers, but this much is clear: there will be a judgment in God's good time.

Secret and Sealed, 12:9.

God revealed to Daniel that the persecution of Antiochus IV would end in three and a half years, but when he pressed God for more, he got nothing. God gives us some answers, but not all we want. The rest we have to take on faith.

Daniel's attempt to pump God for more information is actually a commentary on life. After all, *everyone* wants to know more. Who is a Christian and who is not? That is "secret and sealed." God will let us know at the end. Who truly is in the will of God, and who just thinks they are? Again, that is "secret and sealed." We will find out later. What is exactly right and what is exactly wrong? We will not find out for sure until the end. This is "secret and sealed." Does this mean we know nothing about God? Of course not. We know many things about God. But when it comes to the future, it is mainly "secret and sealed."

This idea is not a marginal biblical concept. Rather, it is the sense of the whole Bible. We know a little about God; we know *enough*. And for the rest, we live by faith. Unfortunately, we live with "certainty merchants," people (mostly preachers) who insist that they "know" the mind of God. They believe that what is hidden even from Daniel, the disciples, and the Apostle Paul is apparent to them. They claim to see through a glass clearly, while Paul saw but "dimly" (1 Cor 13:12a). And since so many are hungry for any word about the future, we let them get away with going beyond the Bible. We are mistaken to tolerate such, for it leads only to disappointment. Then we see evidence of the destructive nature of their rantings: cynicism and a falling away from the faith.

God gave Daniel part of what he wanted to know, and likewise, God does the same for us. But God did not give Daniel answers to all that was going to happen in the future. "Happy are those who persevere and attain the thousand three hundred thirty-five days" (12:12). And the rest was sealed. Daniel had to trust God. But one more personal detail crept into the text: "But you, go your way, and rest; you shall rise for your reward at the end of the days" (12:13). The veil was lifted once again. Daniel will be included among the faithful at the Last Day. The rest of us have to walk by faith.

Notes

Notes

LIVING IN THE MEANTIME

Matthew 24:1-51

Central Question

What should I do while waiting for Christ to return?

Scripture

Matthew 24:32-46 From the fig tree learn its lesson: as soon as its branch becomes tender and puts forth its leaves, you know that summer is near. 33 So also, when you see all these things, you know that he is near, at the very gates. 34 Truly I tell you, this generation will not pass away until all these things have taken place. 35 Heaven and earth will pass away, but my words will not pass away. 36 But about that day and hour no one knows, neither the angels of heaven, nor the Son, but only the Father. 37 For as the days of Noah were, so will be the coming of the Son of Man. 38 For as in those days before the flood they were eating and drinking, marrying and giving in marriage, until the day Noah entered the ark, 39 and they knew nothing until the flood came and swept them all away, so too will be the coming of the Son of Man. 40 Then two will be in the field; one will be taken and one will be left. 41 Two women will be grinding meal together; one will be taken and one will be left. 42 Keep awake therefore, for you do not know on what day your Lord is coming. 43 But understand this: if the owner of the house had known in what part of the night the thief was coming, he would have stayed awake and would not have let his house be broken into. 44 Therefore you also must be ready, for the Son of Man is coming at an unexpected hour. 45 Who then is the faithful and wise slave, whom his master has put in charge of his household, to give the other slaves their allowance of food at the proper time? 46 Blessed is that slave whom his master will find at work when he arrives.

Remembering

Today's Scripture passage takes place during the last week of Jesus' earthly ministry. You will remember that in chapter 21 Jesus had entered Jerusalem and cursed the Fig Tree (21:18-22). In chapter 22 there are various accounts about paying taxes, the Resurrection, and the greatest commandment—all important factors involved in the last week of Jesus' life on earth. Chapter 23 goes on to describe Jesus' all-out attack against the religious leaders, namely the scribes and Pharisees (more specifically, the *controlling* element of the Pharisees). The chapter concludes with Jesus' emotional lament over the city of Jerusalem.

In order to understand chapter 24, however, we must keep in mind the book of Daniel, especially the material covered in the sessions spanning the past two weeks. The vision of the future and the coming of the Son of Man, along with the promise of resurrection, prove to be the foundation of today's passage.

While the "son of man" in Daniel 7 probably was originally intended to signify the angel Michael (Dan 10:13,21; 12:1), the title has been transferred to Jesus. Just as Michael would reign victorious over the "little horn," so now Jesus would demonstrate for his followers that the love and grace he urged could overcome any obstacle.

Studying

(24:1-14) Jesus spent his last week mostly in Jerusalem at the magnificent and glorious temple, the central place of worship and communication in the city. In fact, it was impossible—both literally *and* symbolically—to avoid walking in its shadow. As the disciples gazed upon its splendor, Jesus revealed that one day the temple would be destroyed. Just as it had with the people of

Jeremiah's day, the temple had replaced the worship of *God* with the worship of the *place* itself (Jer 7).

In verse 3, the disciples ask Jesus those same questions that have been on the minds of millions as we anticipate the new millennium: "When will it happen?" "What is the sign of Christ's return?" And perhaps of most interest, "What about the end of the world?" It seems as though we should be excited that Jesus divulged that many would pretend to be the Messiah, wars among the nations would abound, and there would be numerous famines and earthquakes. The only problem is, this description could easily describe *every* generation of human history. His answer was that the end could happen now or in a thousand years. Of course, this was hardly the answer anyone wanted.

In verses 9-14, Jesus notes that persecutions will come, there will be false prophets, and many will be led astray. Do the names Jim Jones, David Koresh, or Heaven's Gate ring any bells? Yet the ultimate truth is embedded in this warning: that the one who would be saved from such pretenders and times of persecutions is "the one who endures to the end." Endurance demands much faith.

The early church taught that Christ would return soon after his resurrection, and even Paul thought Jesus would return before he [Paul] died. Not a single record suggests that the church even entertained the notion that it might be a minimum of two millennia before Christ returned. That being the case, the Gospels were written to offer hope and guidance until Christ's return.

(24:15-31) Jesus warned the people that when they saw the "desolating sacrilege standing in the holy place," they could rest assured that the end would be near. But the "end" of what? In Daniel 9:27 the "desolating sacrilege" was the placement of the statue of Zeus in the temple in Jerusalem. In Jesus' day, however, this was actually *expected* of the ruling Roman emperor. In the 40s Caligula threatened to place his own statue in the Temple, but never actually followed through.

The point is that such turmoil and trouble might very well have awaited the disciples and the church as soon as the coming of the next emperor. In fact, during the years of Nero (AD 54–68), Vespassian (AD 69–79), and Domitian (AD 81–96), Jews and Christians faced various onslaughts of persecution.

"The Book of Daniel was taken as prophecy by later readers who saw the 'abomination of desolation' as a sign which must take place before the end. It is possible that Caligula's attempt to erect his statue in the Temple (40 AD) was taken as a fulfillment of this 'prophecy'" (Mauldin, 4).

However, it was during the reign of Vespassian that his general Titus conquered Jerusalem, which resulted in his capturing and destroying the temple, at which point many wondered, is this the "end"? Probably, they assumed. After all, surely the "end" would involve something going wrong with the temple (going back to vv. 1-8).

A far greater concern for Jesus on behalf of his disciples was the presence of messianic pretenders—those claiming messiahship, doing miraculous things, and leading many "astray." In fact, in verses 29-31 Jesus utters the most "apocalyptic" words in today's text. The cosmic elements of the sun and moon and stars reveal his familiarity with Daniel and Joel. The coming of the Son of Man now refers not to the archangel Michael, as it did in Daniel, but rather to Jesus himself in the event that will bring peace to all who endure the persecutions yet remain faithful.

(24:32-44) But when will it happen? Jesus did not give specifics because he did not know them: "But about that day and hour no one knows, neither the angels of heaven, nor the Son, but only the Father." Why is it, then, that people both in and outside the church have spent the majority of their lives trying to predict when the end will happen? One televangelist, one seminar, and

even one Sunday school class after another have spent countless hours, weeks, months—even lifetimes—trying to sort out the schedule of the end of the world. Plain and simple, this task is a fruitless effort.

Jesus' instructions are very clear. The fig tree he cursed in chapter 21 returns to provide a lesson: as surely as the fig tree produces fruit in its season, so will come the Kingdom of God. Jesus uses a contemporary example to help people understand that everything happens in its proper time. As for the Kingdom, God and God alone has chosen the proper time (24:32-33). The "generation" *did* experience the fall of Jerusalem and the destruction of the temple, but has Jesus returned? Not yet. But that is the lesson of verses 36-44: watch, for the signs are clear, and they are the same for each generation.

(24:45-51) What are we to do? Like faithful slaves who are rewarded for their work, we are likewise rewarded for doing God's work. If we are persistent in these labors, when Christ returns, he will find us doing his work. Would you rather he find you arguing about dates, charts, and timetables for his return, or would you prefer he find you feeding the hungry, clothing the naked, giving water to the thirsty, releasing the captive, and visiting the sick (Mt 25:31-46)?

> When the Son of Man comes in his glory, and all the angels with him, then he will sit on the throne of his glory. All the nations will be gathered before him, and he will separate people one from another as a shepherd separates the sheep from the goats, and he will put the sheep at his right hand and the goats at the left. Then the king will say to those at his right hand, "Come, you that are blessed by my Father, inherit the kingdom prepared for you from the foundation of the world; for I was hungry and you gave me food, I was thirsty and you gave me something to drink, I was a stranger and you welcomed me, I was naked and you gave me clothing, I was sick and you took care of me, I was in prison and you visited me." (Mt 25:31-36)

Understanding

We are obsessed with time, constantly worrying over when such-and-such will happen. But our calendars and watches are not divinely sanctioned. These devices are merely synthetic instruments used for measuring time. Our dates and hours are so unstable in their reliability that the number "2000" ... or "2012" ... could never mean anything other than that it is simply a number.

Even Jesus did not know when he would return. Although he knew all the apocalyptic language and the right things to say, ultimately he never made any predictions regarding the end. In fact, he never even attempted to appear as though he had that information. In other words, what matters is that, like the faithful slave, believers continue to do the work of Christ. If we do, then as sure as a (fig) tree yields fruit in its season, Christ will one day come for those who feed the hungry and clothe the naked.

Christ will indeed come like the "son of man," but not with a sword. Instead, Christ will come with loaves of bread and the hands of healing. We are to do likewise.

What About Me?

• *Beware of false messiahs.* Whether it is David Koresh, Jim Jones, or someone else, we all know of people who have led others astray. Unfortunately, most of the time these pretenders cannot be discerned until after they have ruined the lives of many people. Granted, many pastors and denominational leaders may not have the exposure of Jones or Koresh, but are nonetheless just as dangerous. What is our responsibility in disputing a false messiah's claims?

• *Throw away your "Christ Returns" calendar.* If *Jesus* himself did not know when he would return, then how can *we* possibly know? Instead of studying the charts, study the Word with the help of a responsible Bible class and teacher, so that you may come to know its teachings.

• *What do I do until Christ returns?* The answer is simple: live according to God's will. Love, heal, forgive. Be a peacemaker. Love your family. Stand up against wrongdoing. Stand up against religious authority that does not keep Matthew 25:31-46 at the heart of its teaching. Doing this may bring persecution, because it is a radical gospel by which Jesus calls us to live. But in the true spirit of apocalyptic literature, those who endure will be saved.

Resources

Dennis Duling, "The Gospel According to Matthew," *HarperCollins Study Bible*, ed. Wayne A. Meeks (New York: HarperCollins, 1993) 1901–6.

Frank Mauldin, "Abomination of Desolation," *Mercer Dictionary of the Bible*, ed. Watson E. Mills et al. (Macon GA: Mercer University Press, 1990).

LIVING IN THE MEANTIME
Matthew 24:1-51

Introduction

While the only example of pure apocalyptic literature in the New Testament is Revelation, there are bits and pieces of the apocalyptic in the Gospels. Mark 13 and Matthew 24 (today's text) are illustrations. So think this way: Our subject is Last Things and the style is apocalyptic. The poetic style and symbolism are present, but the dreams and visions are absent.

What Jesus said about the Second Coming and how we are to conduct ourselves during hard times is staple fare for every well-rounded Bible study. When we read, "As Jesus came out of the Temple..." (Mt 24:1a NRSV), we think we are on familiar ground. We pride ourselves on knowing the Gospels, but the truth is that we know them selectively. Today's text is difficult. The flamboyant, entertaining, sometimes dogmatic preacher who tends to hover around "the Second Coming" knows this material well. This kind of preacher claims to know what every verse means, including how it connects to past, present, and future. But that kind of arrogance has turned off most thoughtful people. Further, too many of those people have been wrong too often for us to take them seriously.

Our title is "Living in the Meantime." Before the Second Coming, there will be an interim during which the Church will do her work. The early Church thought the "in-between time" would be short, but they were wrong. We *still* live in the "in-between time." This session tells us how we are to live in an extended "in-between time."

I've studied this material longer than usual, but I have not been able to make all of the themes of Matthew 24 fit neatly into a pattern. The parts of the text I don't understand, I will leave alone. The parts I do understand, I will try to package in a way that you can use. There are two sections in my "comment": the teachings and the applications.

There is a lot of material in this chapter, so do not feel as if you need to cover it all. Surely it's better to get one bite and chew it well than to give more than can be swallowed.

The Teachings

(1) Jerusalem will fall. "As Jesus came out of the Temple and was going away, his disciples came to point out to him the buildings of the Temple" (24:1). They were impressive! Frank Stagg wrote of the Temple, "The buildings were of white marble and were decorated with gold, precious stones, and rich tapestries. The Temple was one of the wonders of the world" (*The Broadman Commentary*, vol. 8, Nashville: Broadman Press, 1969, 216).

First-century Jews became so proud, so impressed with their Temple, that they lost sight of its purpose, until the building actually replaced God as the first object of their adoration. But Jesus condemned the Jewish system on an even deeper level. It had become so corrupt in leadership, so misguided in theology, so blind to mission, until it simply had to go.

"Truly I tell you, not one stone will be left here upon another; all will be thrown down" (24:2b). And it happened just as Jesus said it would. In AD 70, the Roman general Titus led an army in the conquest and destruction of Jerusalem.

(2) Pretenders will arise. "Beware that no one leads you astray. For many will come in my name, saying, 'I am the Messiah!' and they will lead many astray" (24:4-5). The same idea is repeated in 24:11. And still a third time, Jesus says, "Then if anyone says to you, 'Look! Here is the Messiah!' or 'There he is!'—do not believe it. For false messiahs and false prophets will appear...to lead astray, if possible, even the elect" (24:23-24).

Life is hard and confusing, and to be honest, sometimes it just doesn't make sense. Then along comes somebody who acts and talks as if they have all the answers. And as sure as sunup, a crowd will gather around this individual who claims to have the last word from God. David Koresh and Jim Jones come to mind.

In the last 20 years, simple, devout, misled people have followed Koresh and Jones to death. In fact, just a couple of years ago, seemingly intelligent people in California committed suicide at the command of their leader. Jesus warns against false messiahs.

We have a Messiah. He came as a babe in a manger, lived among us as a carpenter, taught us, died for us, and lives again by the will of God. Not only has this Messiah left instructions about how we are to live, but also he has promised to come for us at the Last Day. We don't need another messiah; we have *The* Messiah.

(3) Pagans will persecute. "They will hand you over to be tortured and will put you to death, and you will be hated by all nations because of my name" (24:9). Intermittently for two thousand years, Christians have been persecuted. Strangely, sometimes the persecution has come from others who called themselves Christians. Today in Indonesia, Iran, Algeria, and China, there is great risk in being a Christian. In Iran you can be thrown into prison without a moment's notice. In China, Christians are limited in that government consent must be obtained to print a Bible, open a church, or speak publicly about Christ. Keith Parks remarks that more Christians have been killed for their faith in the twentieth century than in the first. This text seems remote to us, because we don't know the limits to religious liberty in other parts of the world. Isn't it ironic that in places where Christians are harassed and imprisoned, the faith seems to flower? The Church in China is a prime example.

It may be that the Church could endure outright persecution better than being ignored. Europe and North America may be subjecting the Church to a more severe test. Can we stand prosperity and cultural snubbing? Both are left-handed contempt and have the effect of persecution.

(4) Christians will divide. "And many false prophets will arise and lead many astray. And because of the increase of lawlessness, the love of many will grow cold. But the one who endures to the end will be saved" (24:11-13). It is no wonder that many people fall away from practicing their faith. Our culture sends not one signal but many, and the "signs" are confusing. Preachers do not all concur, and consequently, send conflicting messages. Too many Christians set poor examples. An easy lifestyle seduces

many. And the result? "The love of many will grow cold" (24:12b). And it has.

The temptation is to give up on organized religion altogether and do our own thing. Jesus anticipated this, saying, "But the one who endures to the end will be saved" (24:11). When we come to the "end of our ropes," we're supposed to tie a knot and hang on—hang onto our faith, our faith patterns (going to church, studying Scripture, praying, tithing), and most of all, our hope.

(5) Signs will confuse. There are signs throughout Matthew 24. Some of these anticipate the fall of Jerusalem (24:15-22). Others are about the end of the world and the Second Coming. Sorting out which is which is hard. Those consumed with the Second Coming have combed these verses searching for clues. Most have gone beyond good interpretation. Trying to "read" these signs is uncertain work.

• "For nation will rise against nation, and kingdom against kingdom, and there will be famines and earthquakes in various places: all this is but the beginning of the birth pangs" (24:7-8). Obviously, these *signs*—earthquakes, famines, wars—have occurred repeatedly throughout history. Does this mean the end is at hand? The dilemma is blatant: the serious interpreter is confused and the door is open to the charlatan.

• "Truly I tell you, this generation will not pass away until all these things have taken place" (24:34). I cannot explain this passage. Apparently, Jesus is suggesting that all the "signs" that were mentioned in Matthew 24 would come to pass and that the Second Coming would be in the lifetime of the disciples. That never happened. Critics of Christianity have hurried to label this passage a clear instance in which Jesus was wrong (George Bernard Shaw referenced this "error" in his debates with G. K. Chesterton). However, I don't believe Jesus erred.

• Speculation about the Second Coming never ends. Jesus deemed such speculation wasted time: "But about that day and hour no one knows, neither the angels of heaven, nor the Son, but only the Father" (24:36). If *Jesus* didn't know the date of the Second Coming, doesn't it seem foolish for a preacher or teacher to claim that knowledge?

(6) Jesus *will* come again. Two parts of our text address this subject:

• "And this good news of the kingdom will be proclaimed throughout the world, as a testimony to all the nations; and then the end will come" (24:14). It is as if Jesus were saying, "When everyone has heard God's good news, then the end will come." Considering this, perhaps we can have a hand in hurrying Jesus' return through missions.

• "Immediately after the suffering of those days...then the sign of the Son of Man will appear in heaven...and they will see the Son of Man coming on the clouds of heaven with power and great glory" (24:29-30).

I have tried to address the themes of the Second Coming with some regularity throughout my ministry, but always they have been mysterious and difficult. We must remember, however, that the Second Coming is not "tacked onto" the Gospel; it is at the very heart of it, and we should not avoid studying about it. God is in control of history. As God sent God's Son once, so will the Son come again to tie together the loose ends of history and morality with a great judgment. It's the only way this tangled world will ever make sense.

The Applications

(1) Stay the course. "The one who endures to the end will be saved" (24:13). More than likely, Matthew was written during a time of persecution. There is always the temptation to abandon Christ—and indeed all that is Christian—and just try to save your own skin. Jesus anticipated this flight reaction to hard times, and he counseled endurance, staying the course. This may be the word some of us need today.

(2) Avoid the extremes. When false claims are made (and some are well-intended), don't believe them. When strange, crazy predictions are made about Last Things, ignore them. When someone claims to know more than Jesus does, that person likely will mislead you in other areas as well.

(3) Do missions. One legitimate part of hurrying the Kingdom of God is missions (see 24:14), which most churches have incorporated into their ministries. This text suggests we do more.

(4) Be ready. Our text ends with two illustrations about readiness for the coming of Christ (24:36-44 and 24:45-51). The sense of both is being ready, for no one knows when the end will come. I certainly don't claim to know how the end of the world will come, though I do know how the end came for my father. It was a surprise. He was taken by a stroke. One day he was up and around, and the next he was in the hospital and gone. His end came "as a thief in the night." So the text applies to my father: "Therefore you also must be ready, for the Son of Man is coming at an unexpected hour" (24:44). That's the way Jesus came for Dad, and I suspect that's the way he will come for me. I need to be ready.

Notes

_____

_____

_____

_____

_____

_____

_____

_____

_____

_____

_____

_____

_____

_____

_____

Notes

GIVING AN
ACCOUNT
Revelation 20:11–21:8

Central Question

How can I prepare for a time when I will stand before God?

Scripture

Revelation 20:11-15 Then I saw a great white throne and the one who sat on it; the earth and the heaven fled from his presence, and no place was found for them. 12 And I saw the dead, great and small, standing before the throne, and books were opened. Also another book was opened, the book of life. And the dead were judged according to their works, as recorded in the books. 13 And the sea gave up the dead that were in it, Death and Hades gave up the dead that were in them, and all were judged according to what they had done. 14 Then Death and Hades were thrown into the lake of fire. This is the second death, the lake of fire; 15 and anyone whose name was not found written in the book of life was thrown into the lake of fire.

21:1-5 Then I saw a new heaven and a new earth; for the first heaven and the first earth had passed away, and the sea was no more. 2 And I saw the holy city, the new Jerusalem, coming down out of heaven from God, prepared as a bride adorned for her husband. 3 And I heard a loud voice from the throne saying, "See, the home of God is among mortals. He will dwell with them as their God; they will be his peoples, and God himself will be with them; 4 he will wipe every tear from their eyes. Death will be no more; mourning and crying and pain will be no more, for the first things have passed away." 5 And the one who was seated on the throne said, "See, I am making all things new." Also he said, "Write this, for these words are trustworthy and true."

Remembering

Before going any further, read the entire book of Revelation in one sitting. Although it may take you two or three hours to finish, your time will be well spent. Once you have done this, you will more than likely realize that the importance of this book is not in the minute details. After all, can you remember what every trumpet or bowl represents? Of course not. Neither could the original audience of this book. They did not debate over who the 144,000 people were, because they knew that this figure implied a variation of the number 12 (not only the number of tribes in ancient Israel, but also the number of disciples). Revelation was not intended to be taken literally, but instead, figuratively. If the book's original audience did not debate over when Christ would return, then why are *we* so absorbed with such a futile endeavor?

The numbers "12" and "7" are often used figuratively in Scripture.

By combing the entire book in one sitting, you can realize just how figurative Revelation really is. John has just been banished to Patmos during the persecutions under Domitian, the emperor of Rome (AD 81–96). Although these persecutions were not wide-spread, they were still pervasive. While on the island, John receives visions (in typical apocalyptic form) of angels, beasts, messengers riding on horseback, a young pregnant woman, and even the spirits of darkness. The number "666" was spec-ulated to be a reference to Nero, a tyrant under whom

In the Bible, the well-known "666" of Revelation 13:18 is the only clear example of using numbers to refer to something understood only by a few. This is actually the sum of numerical values assigned to the letters of a particular human name, "Nero" being among the many suggestions. The Hebrew transcription of the Greek form of his name, which would equal the value 666, is attested in a scroll from Murabba'at; moreover, the Hebrew transcription of the Latin form of his name would explain the variant reading "616" in some manuscripts (Wiles, 622).

terrible persecutions took place (some believe the numerical value of the name Caesar Nero adds up to 666), and the author probably saw Domitian as the "return" of Nero. Whether you understand the book as a play for the stage of Ephesus (Blevins) or as a standard apocalypse (Aune), you will certainly be left with one thought: God is in control and will deliver the faithful.

Studying

Before the Throne of God (20:11-15) Following the passages detailing the millennial Kingdom (20:4-6) and the defeat of Satan (20:7-10), John sees a vision in which the graves "give up the dead," and he watches as they proceed to a "great white throne" where they are to be judged.

Two books are then opened: the Book of Life, and another which apparently contains the names of those not listed in the Book of Life. The Book of Life, "a heavenly registry of the names of God's people, a metaphor for salvation and election" (Aune, 2335), is noted in Revelation as containing the names of the faithful, those who endure to the end (see 3:5; 13:8; 17:8; 20:15; 21:27). The Book of Life concept is not new for John. In fact, it is as old as Moses. In Exodus 32:32, when God is about to destroy the people who have built the golden calf, Moses intercedes on their behalf by insisting that God either forgive them or "blot me out of the book that you have written." While names are not "blotted out" as such, with this proposal Moses was indicating that he would rather sacrifice himself than see the people destroyed. In this way, he interceded for them as a prophet would do.

The Book of Life is also the subject of Daniel 12:1 (see lesson for Jan 16), Luke 10:20, and Philippians 4:3. The text in Luke is especially worth noting. Jesus has already sent the 70 out for a mission and they have just returned (Lk 10:1-12, 17-20). Just after the "apocalyptic" comment that he saw "Satan fall from heaven," Jesus tells the 70 that they should rejoice, because their "names are written in heaven." John comforts his readers by writing in Revelation 12 that the red dragon flees heaven and takes a third of the stars with him only to be defeated by Michael and his angels. As frightening as the text seems, John's intention is to assure his readers of God's ultimate control. Does this remind you of our discussion on Daniel 7 three weeks ago?

But what does it all mean? Good question. While verses 13-15 tell us that in John's vision the good are rewarded to eternal life, the bad are thrown into the lake of fire. As with our discussion of Daniel 12, the importance of this

> The seventy returned with joy, saying, "Lord, in your name even the demons submit to us!" He said to them, "I watched Satan fall from heaven like a flash of lightning. See, I have given you authority to tread on snakes and scorpions, and over all the power of the enemy; and nothing will hurt you. Nevertheless, do not rejoice at this, that the spirits submit to you, but rejoice that your names are written in heaven." (Lk 10:17-20)

text is not found in the details. If one is faithful to God, the future is resurrection to eternal life. Will it happen exactly as John saw it? Another good question. The answer: we cannot know for sure; neither are we supposed to know. Apocalyptic literature is not concerned with *how* things happen, only that they *will* happen. For the one who is faithful and does the will of God, there is eternal life. Doing God's will should be our only concern, not what will happen if we do not.

The New Heaven and New Earth (21:1-4) Unlike other biblical books that were meant to be read or heard, Revelation must be *experienced*—with both the imagination and the senses. The writer uses different systems of symbols: numbers, colors, animals—even places take on symbolic meaning.

Read these four verses and understand the tone or emotion of what awaits those listed in the Book of Life. After experiencing the imagery of a new heaven and new earth from Isaiah 65:17 (see Isa 43:19), John understands the beauty of resurrection and eternal life.

Drama was very popular in Ancient Greece. Aeschylus, Sophocles, and Euripides were among the most popular playwrights of their day and time. Greek drama was still popular in Asia Minor in the first century. The theater was basic entertainment and the hottest ticket in town.

Imagine that we live in the first century and that the book of Revelation was written to be performed as a play on the stage. One night we arrive at the theater to see the latest play. The playwright is a Christian named John and he has called his play *The Apocalypse*. As the play unfolds, we see John, some heavenly figures, some beasts, all kinds of monsters and plagues, and a terrible battle in which God emerges victorious. It is a bit confusing. What are we to think?

After the play, we meet this new playwright, who tells us in secret that the victory in the show actually symbolizes victory over the Roman empire, and that all those who remain faithful to God will be saved. "Will all of those things really happen?" asks a young man. "No, of course not," John would reply. "Don't take it so literally. But in one way or another, we will all stand accountable before God's throne for the lives we have lived." Revelation is like a profound movie. Its images are meant to convey thoughts, feelings, and truths. Some would say, then, that Revelation is a horror movie, others that it is an action movie. Still others might dub it as a dramatic comedy. After all, though dramatic and sad, it also radiates with great victory and joy.

The Alpha and the Omega (21:5-8) Verse 5 is rooted in the great prophecy of Isaiah 65:17-25. According to this passage, God creates a new heaven and a new earth, restoring Jerusalem following the Babylonian Exile. The vision is one of peace and tranquility, culminating in the great scene of "peace on earth" in verse 25: "The wolf and lamb shall feed together, The lion shall eat straw like the ox." Such is life in heaven.

These words are not just poetic and visionary, but according to the author, they are "trustworthy and true" as well (v. 5b). That is because they originate with Jesus Christ, the "Alpha and the Omega." "Alpha" is the first letter of the Greek alphabet, while "Omega" is

the last (see Rev 1:8), just as Jesus Christ is the beginning and end of all things (Isa 44:6). Verses 7-8 clarify what happens to those who "conquer" and those who are "cowardly." The "cowardly" are those who fall beneath the weight of persecution. When their faith is tested, they deny Christ. On the other hand, those who "conquer" will be the "children" of God.

Understanding

To say that we all will "go to the throne of God" is another way of declaring ourselves accountable for everything we do. We must be more concerned with doing God's work than with trying to figure out what the seven candlesticks in Revelation mean. Jesus said that each Christian should strive to be like the obedient slave (Mt 24:45-51). What an analogy!

Even now, with millennial fervor mounting and people increasingly becoming more intimidated, it is easy to lose sight of our primary task: following Jesus' teachings. Rather than spending "God's time" trying to figure out the details of Revelation (or Daniel), we should be more concerned with helping those who need food and clothing, healing and forgiveness, release and grace.

See Jesus' words in Matthew 24–25 and last week's lesson.

For just a moment, pretend that tomorrow every book ever printed will be burned, including Bibles. Now, suppose you are allowed to keep only one page of any book you choose, one page that will be the only reading material available to the next generation. What would your page have on it? Would it be a page from the Bible? From Shakespeare? Would it be a recipe? Would it be from the *TV Guide*?

My choice would be the page from the Gospel of Matthew containing 25:31-46. Why? Because by reading this passage alone, you can discover God's will for your life. In fact, it contains the very words that take you "to the throne of God," the words that can revolutionize societies, change lives, and topple governments. That's *my* choice. What's yours? Regardless, reading and knowing cover only certain aspects of God's will. Ultimately, though, one has to *act*. When the day of judgment comes, wouldn't it be best if God were to find you busy feeding, clothing, and housing those who have nothing? Apocalyptic literature does not look past the present to the future; rather, it equips us to see how life in the present enables us to have a future at all.

What About Me?

• *Do.* Asking ourselves the popular catch phrase "What would Jesus do?" is the wrong approach. Instead, we should encourage both ourselves and others to "*do* what Jesus did." Anyone can *ask*, but only the faithful *do*.

• *How can I ensure that my name is "written in the Book of Life"?* Follow Christ. It's that simple. Unfortunately—and ironically—it's also that difficult. It is very easy to become caught up in the world, but living by what Christ taught is the key. Read the Gospels repeatedly. Jesus said that the greatest commandment is to love God and our neighbor (this includes your enemies), not to figure out the details of the book of Revelation. Standing before the throne—however it happens—will be a great moment for the "faithful slave."

• *Ultimately, we are all held accountable for our actions and decisions.* The primary purpose of the Bible, however, is to call us to experience an intimate relationship with a God of love, mercy, and grace (Boring, 212). How is *your* relationship with God?

Resource

David Aune, "Revelation: Introduction and Notes," *HarperCollins Study Bible*, ed. Wayne A. Meeks (New York: HarperCollins, 1993).

James Blevins, "Revelation, Book of," *Mercer Dictionary of the Bible*, ed. Watson Mills (Macon: Mercer University Press, 1991).

John Keating Wiles, "Numbers/Numerology," *Mercer Dictionary of the Bible*, ed. Watson Mills (Macon: Mercer University Press, 1991).

GIVING AN
ACCOUNT
Revelation 20:11–21:8

Introduction

There are two accounts of Judgment Day in the Scripture. The first, in which Jesus tells about the "sheep and goats judgment," is found in Matthew 25:31-46. The second, "the great white throne judgment," is our text for today. We live in a society that gives little thought to Judgment Day. In fact, the whole idea of judgment often is merely dismissed by moderns. Even church people frequently are unable to pronounce judgment on obvious, egregious sin. We know from the Bible that we are not supposed to judge (Mt 7:1-5), but the same Bible also teaches accountability.

Jesus told stories about accountability. Before going away for a while, a master gave his servants talents: five, three, and one respectively. While he was gone, the servants were expected to make good use of their time and talents. When the master returned, he asked each servant to give an account (Mt 25:14-30). If Jesus himself repeatedly taught that stewardship is the prime ingredient to life, and that all will be called to account at the Last Day, then surely the Church ought to repeat the words of Jesus.

Dr. Ray Summers gives us a warning about this kind of lesson: "About the most difficult thing in the New Testament to work into a harmonious system is the body of Scriptures having to do with death, the interim between death and the resurrection, the resurrection, and the judgment" (*Worthy Is the Lamb*, Nashville: Broadman Press, 1951, 210). Preachers who try to work out all the bits and pieces in the Bible on these subjects usually come to a near fixation on Last Things. The Bible is a wonderfully balanced book of many dimensions and subjects. We who teach the Bible need to be both faithful to what the Bible teaches and as balanced as the Bible is.

Dr. Summers goes on to say, "When one sees all the confusion that arises in trying to work out the eschatology of the New Testament, he is inclined to believe that the Lord has a reason for leaving it that way....There are some things man does not need to know, and he must be satisfied to let it remain in the knowledge of God alone" (Ibid., 211). In other words, we don't have to understand exactly how the Second Coming will happen, how Judgment Day will be carried out, or precisely who is going to heaven and who is not.

John was on Patmos, an island used as a prison in the Aegean Sea. Probably he was sentenced to Patmos for refusing to swear allegiance to the emperor. While a prisoner for Christ's sake, he received visions which make up the book of Revelation (the only example of pure apocalyptic literature in the New Testament). In grand style, John lines out the Last Things and final victory for Christ's people—a truly appropriate end to Scripture. Rome was persecuting Christians, but into the suffering came this message of hope. The bottom-line message of the book is that in the end, God would take care of God's people, allowing truth and justice to triumph.

God Is Judge, 20:11a.

"Then I saw a great white throne and the one who sat on it..." (Rev 20:11a NRSV). In John's vision God was the one who came to judge us all. The Gospels speak on the contrary: "The Father judges no one but has given all judgment to the Son, so that all may honor the Son just as they honor the Father" (Jn 5:22-23a). (Other New Testament texts that tell of Jesus' judging humankind are in Mt 25:31-46, Acts 17:31, and 2 Tim 4:1.) This "difficulty" is a small one. After all, the same Paul who said in Acts 17:31 that Jesus would judge the world also said, "Why do you despise your brother or sister? For we will all stand before the judgment seat of God" (Rom 14:10). Perhaps William Barclay sheds some light on the subject with his comment, "The unity of the Father and the Son is such that there is no difficulty in ascribing the action of the one to the other" (*The Revelation of John*, vol. 2, Philadelphia: Westminster Press, 1976, 195).

The "white throne" is a picture of a holy and perfect justice that only God can dispense. God knows the evidence, God knows how to make a true verdict, and only God can decide between heaven and hell for us all. God, who will sit upon "a great white throne," is qualified to judge. Judgment from God is not cruel or vindictive. It is, in fact, the only avenue to making moral sense of the world we live in.

Time Is Up, 20:11a.

This passage teaches that there will finally come an "end of the world": "The earth and the heaven fled from his presence; and no place was found for them" (20:11b). Peter said the same thing, only using different words: "But the day of the Lord will come like a thief, and then the heavens will pass away with a loud noise, and the elements will be dissolved with fire, and the earth and everything that is done on it will be disclosed" (2 Pet 3:10).

The God who began it all eons ago finally will decide that *time is no more*! Nothing is more predictable than sunup and sundown. But the Bible teaches that there will come a time when God will call a halt to the natural order. Mark quotes Jesus: "Heaven and earth will pass away..." (Mk 13:31). The same idea appears in Psalm 102:25-27 and 2 Peter 3:10. All of this seems strange to us, but Christians believe that what appears constant is really passing. Those things that seem farfetched actually are the only things that are going to last. But when this earth passes away, God has another one prepared. Barclay put it well when he said, "The new man in Christ must have a new world in Christ" (Barclay, 195).

All Are Present, 20:12a and 13.

"And I saw the dead, great and small, standing before the throne..." (20:12a). The same theme reappears later in the text: "And the sea gave up the dead that were in it, Death and Hades gave up the dead that were in them, and all were judged according to what they had done" (20:13).

• "The dead, great and small, standing before the throne..." The value given a person in this world will not affect final judgment. No one is so insignificant that they can obtain a "pass" on judgment. Neither is anyone so important that they will be excused from judgment. All will be made equal at Judgment Day.

• "And the sea gave up the dead that were in it, Death and Hades gave up the dead that were in them, and all were judged..." In the ancient world, a proper burial was considered vital to the spirit of the deceased. In our text, "the accidents of death will not prevent any from appearing before the judge" (H. B. Swete, quoted in Barclay, 197).

Everybody is going to be there. Regardless of our opinions on judgment, the God who made us has scheduled a time to settle accounts, and all will keep this appointment.

Books Are Opened, 20:12-13.

Two kinds of books are kept. The idea of God's keeping books runs throughout the Bible. From Daniel 7:10b ("The court sat in judgment, and the books were opened.") throughout the inter-biblical period, the Jews were taught that God was watching and that a constant record was being kept. So, in Jewish texts with which we are somewhat unfamiliar—like Enoch, The Apocalypse of Baruch, and 2 Baruch—reference is made to God's bookkeeping. The Church of the Middle Ages developed a fear theology from these texts. For instance, a great eye is painted atop one of the chapels in Rome. The message is hard to miss: God is above us, watching and recording all we do in this life.

Our ideas about God have changed since the Middle Ages. We see God as loving, forgiving—a Friend. Considering this, I think we've moved in the right direction. But don't forget the books. Again, there are two kinds:

(1) One is a book of deeds: "All were judged according to what they had done" (20:13b). Many of us like to believe that "works" have little to do with salvation; we take comfort in knowing that we are saved by grace. But both judgment scenes in the New Testament place a high priority on "works." According to the "sheep-and-goats" judgment of Matthew, salvation depends upon how we treat the sick, hungry, naked, and imprisoned. Paul soft-

ens this "works" theology, but he doesn't dismiss it. I think our salvation depends on what we do with Jesus as well as how we treat the weak and needy. Since the Scripture cites both, shouldn't our theology likewise incorporate both? Morris Ashcraft connects the Jesus-oriented part of our faith with the part our deeds play in our salvation, saying, "The first standard simply stresses the stewardship of life: man is judged on the basis of what he did with what he had in life. The second standard involves all the faith and decision through which one goes in declaring himself for God" (Clifton J. Allen, ed., *The Broadman Commentary*, vol. 12, Nashville: Broadman Press, 1972, 351).

(2) The second book is "the Book of Life." Again, this phrase appears often (see Ex 32:32; Isa 4:3; Phil 4:3; Rev 13:8). Ray Summers ties the two kinds of books together: "If any man's name was not found in the book of life, the records in the books of works condemned him and he was cast in the lake of fire" (Summers, 210).

In a sense, we are writing our own destinies by the way we live. God's history with humanity has involved God's honoring our choices. If we choose no relationship, God will not "force" us, although God does leave the door open. According to Jesus, those who choose the narrow path, who choose to be in a constant, working, growing relationship with God and God's community, reap the benefits of what God has to offer.

Death Is No More, 20:14.

"Then Death and Hades were thrown into the lake of fire. This is the second death, the lake of fire..." (20:14-15a). In Revelation 20:10, one verse before our text of the day begins, there is this statement: "And the devil who had deceived them was thrown into the lake of fire...." Now Death and Hades are thrown into the same "lake of fire." In a way, we seem to have lost, for the writers of the New Testament tie Devil and Death together. But Paul writes of Jesus' final victory, "When this perishable body puts on imperishability, and this mortal body puts on immortality, then the saying that is written will be fulfilled: Death has been swallowed up in victory. Where, O death, is your victory? Where, O death, is your sting? The sting of death is sin, and the power of sin is the law. But thanks be to God, who gives us the victory through our Lord Jesus Christ" (1 Cor 54-57).

John had a final vision of the New Jerusalem: "He will wipe away every tear from their eyes. Death will be no more; mourning and crying and pain will be no more, for the first things have passed away" (21:4). This is what it will be like "on the other side." Now we are one with Isaiah, who wrote of God's tomorrow, "The wolf shall live with the lamb, the leopard shall lie down with the kid, the calf and the lion and the fatling together, and a little child shall lead them.... For the earth will be full of the knowledge of the Lord as the waters cover the sea" (Isa 11:6, 9).

The vision these saints had of what it would be like when "Death is no more" is hard for us to imagine. But from Genesis 3 until Revelation, God's plan is in the works to erase Eden's damage. Devil and Death, sin and all manner of wickedness will be no more. God in Christ fought against Death and the Devil, and after Christ triumphed, God disposed of them. This is theology on a wide canvas. What a picture! And what a prospect it is for all those who love the Lord and look forward to his return.

Notes

Notes

nextsunday
STUDIES

1 Peter
Keep Hope Alive

This study of First Peter focuses on keeping hope alive in the face of pressures and circumstances that could possibly extinguish it completely, or worse, turn authentic faith into a pale replica of the real thing.

Advent Virtues

The phrase "holiday rush" is not an exaggeration. The frantic pace required to purchase gifts, bake holiday foods, and attend Christmas parties, plays, and performances takes its toll; we arrive at Christmas Day exhausted. Within the context of December busyness, the ancient Christian season of Advent takes on new meaning and acquires renewed importance. May God instill the virtues of *hope*, *peace*, *joy*, *love*, and *faith* in each of us this Advent.

Apocalyptic Literature

This study examines five apocalyptic texts in the Bible—from Zechariah, Daniel, Matthew, and Revelation. With each new year bringing a new prediction of impending doom, it is always a perfect time to get the story straight. Apocalyptic literature does not address the future. It addresses our present.

Approaching a Missional Mindset

The World isn't the same as it once was. We must be the church in a new place, in unimagined ways, and with a wider range of people. Engage your small group with the radical and refreshing challenge of developing a "missional lifestyle."

Baptist Freedom
Celebrating Our Baptist Heritage
What makes a Baptist a Baptist? Of course, the ultimate answer is simple: membership in a local Baptist church. But there are all kinds of Baptist churches! What are the spiritual and theological marks of a Baptist? What is the shape and the feel of Baptist Christianity?

The Bible and the Arts
God has used artistic expression throughout the centuries to convey truth, offer blessing, and urge believers to deeper faithfulness. In modern life, artistic expression flourishes, from movies to books to music to paintings to photographs. Sometimes artists are intentional about trying to portray God's truths. Other times, perhaps God is working even when the artist is unaware of it. As believers, we may hear and see God at work in many art forms.

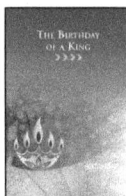

The Birthday of a King
The first four lessons in this unit draw inspiration from a traditional interpretation of the Advent candles as the Prophets' Candle, the Bethlehem Candle, the Shepherds' Candle, and the Angels' Candle. The final lesson, which occurs after Advent, celebrates the theological meaning of Jesus' birth as described in the prologue to John's Gospel.

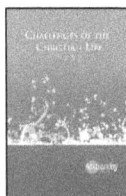

Challenges of the Christian Life
The way of the cross is difficult, and taking Jesus seriously means looking honestly at how we fall short of God's best hopes for us and seeing how much we need God's grace. For all of us there are times when we need to remember that Christ is our saving grace and recommit ourselves to the journey of faith, rediscovering, again and again, the life-giving purpose described in the book of Ephesians.

Christ Is Born!
Even in the midst of difficult circumstances, Advent is a time when we can find hope. Much like today, people in the 1st century church faced struggles. Examining the Gospel of Matthew, lessons include "Waiting for Christ," "Preparing for Christ," "Expecting Christ," "Announcing Christ," and "The Arrival of Christ."

Christians and Hunger

These sessions challenge us to apply gospel lenses and holy imagination to what literally gives us energy to live: food. With God's grace, we have the opportunity to imagine communities where tables are large and all are fed.

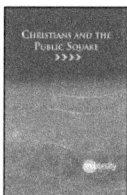

Christians and the Public Square

Politics and faith are tricky areas for Christians to negotiate. The First Amendment to the Constitution guarantees religious freedom for all Americans. As Christians who are also citizens, questions abound: How do we distinguish between faithful and unfaithful forms of civic engagement? How do we give Caesar his due while giving our all to God?

Christmas in Mark

In the early chapters of Mark, we will encounter a Christmas story. This story, however, will not be quite like the one told by other Gospel writers, but it will resonate with the reality of your life. Mark doesn't deny the beauty or reality of the nativity; however, he seems to believe that Christmas begins—the gospel begins—when Christ intrudes upon the hard realities of life.

The Church on a Mission

What does it mean to be a church on a mission? The lesson of Acts 1:8 is that we must simultaneously carry out Christ's mandate at home, in our region, in places that have been our blind spots, and around the world.

Colossians
Living the Faith Faithfully

Paul's letter to the Colossians begins with a high-minded philosophical defense of the faith, but concludes with a collection of extremely practical advice for living by faith. This study addresses the questions many Christians face today, helping them apply Paul's practical advice in their own lives.

Easter Confessions

Easter confession is often found on many different lips in the Gospel of John. When we listen carefully, those ancient confessions still echo into this new millennium.

Embracing the Word of God

We live during a time of transition in Christian history. Basic assumptions about the truth of the Christian faith are being questioned, not only by nonbelievers, but by Christians themselves. First John offers a starting point for understanding of what it means to "be" Christian.

Esther: A Woman of Discretion and Valor

The book of Esther is not a record of historical facts as such. Rather, it is a magnificent narrative that refuses to interpret life as being driven by coincidence or happenstance. In the otherwise unknown characters of Esther, Haman, and Mordecai, we trace the movement of the divine hand as God collaborates with God's risk-taking people to rescue them from the hand of their enemies.

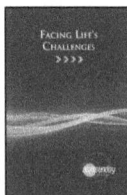

Facing Life's Challenges

This study explores four significant challenges common to most persons of faith: the challenge of new light, the challenge of time's limit, the challenge of living with mystery, and the challenge of authentic spirituality. Although these issues are neither simple nor easy to ponder, this study effectively leads us in confronting these challenges.

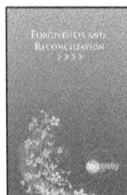

Forgiveness and Reconciliation

Forgiveness is a central issue in our capacity to remain redemptively connected to those relationships we prize. Restoring broken or interrupted relationships is a primary issue for all of us, and managing forgiveness is crucial to the possibility of experiencing reconciliation. Several dimensions of forgiveness affect our lives in significant ways. In this study, we attempt to address a few of those important issues.

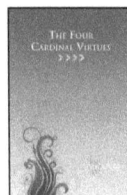

The Four Cardinal Virtues

Christians are learning how to distinguish between members of a church and disciples of Christ. Discipleship involves developing virtues in those who come to our churches seeking life, salvation, grace, mercy. If we want to have something to offer a world in desperate need, then we must return to virtues like discernment, justice, courage, and moderation. We must return to the hard and glorious work of making disciples.

Godly Leadership

Nehemiah was called to return to Jerusalem to lead in the sacred task of rebuilding the city's walls. Displaying characteristics often lacking in secular leadership—prayerful humility, a willingness to work with diverse teams, wisdom in confronting conflict, and a passion to stand with the powerless—Nehemiah offered his people a portrait of godly leadership that can still shape our own calls to lead nearly 2,500 years later.

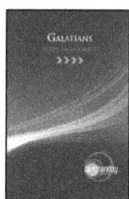

Galatians
Freedom in Christ

Paul wrote with fiery passion, as you will notice from the opening paragraphs of this letter to the Galatians. But his language reveals that he was writing about a crucially important issue—the very nature of salvation in Christ.

A Holy and Surprising Birth

Christmas begins here—discover these five love stories from the book of Luke and renew your appreciation of God's laborious effort to birth our salvation.

How Does the Church Decide?

An array of decisions draw energy and time from church members. These decisions may be theological, such as mode of baptism, aesthetic, such as the color of the sanctuary carpet, or functional, such as the selection of a new minister. This study will consider how the church has made its decisions in the past to help guide our decisions today.

Is God Calling?

Witness the varying forms of God's call, the variety of people called, and the variety of responses. Perhaps God's call to you will become clearer.

James
Gaining True Wisdom
If we'll be honest with God and ourselves as we study what James says, we can make great strides toward wisdom and a living faith.

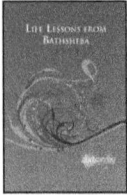

Life Lessons from Bathsheba
Who was Bathsheba? She was a complex figure who developed from the silent object of David's lust into a powerful, vocal, and influential queen mother.

Life Lessons from David
In the Bible, we catch David in the various stages of the human journey: childhood, adolescence, adulthood, and senior adulthood. From the biblical treatment of the stages of David's life, we can land some insights to assist us in better understanding the human journey.

The Matriarchs
The matriarchs of Genesis offer their lives as a testimony of faith, perseverance, and audacity. We learn from their mistakes and suffering. We will gain the hope of Hagar, the joy of Sarah, and the audacity of Rebekah as we are challenged to examine our prejudices and our insecurities while studying Esau and Jacob's wives.

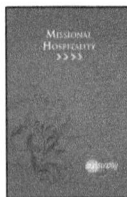

Missional Hospitality
If we are serious about following Jesus, we will be people of open hearts, open hands, and open homes. In other words, as followers of Jesus we will practice the fine art of hospitality. In lesson one, we reflect on hospitality to strangers. In lesson two, we address hospitality to the poor. In lesson three, we focus on hospitality to sinners. In lesson four, we learn about hospitality to newcomers. Lesson five reminds us about our hospitality to Christ.

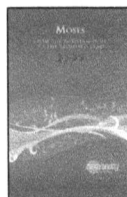

Moses
From the Burning Bush to the Promised Land
We would do well to trace the life of Moses so we might discover how his life changed, both personally and as Israel's leader, as he learned what it meant to love God with all his heart, soul, and strength.

Old Testament Promises to God

Some individuals may feel that our promises couldn't possibly mean anything to God. Perhaps the real question is this: under what circumstances should or do we make such promises? The Old Testament contains several examples of people making promises to God, using the unique form of a biblical "vow."

The Passion of Christ

The four lessons in this unit highlight the faith struggles of the early disciples. In lesson one, Jesus addresses the issues of faith and practice. In lesson two, we meet Judas who, like us, struggled with God's Kingdom and human kingdoms. In lesson three, the issue of temptation reminds us that our faith journey is a constant challenge. Lesson Four invites us to remember Peter's experience of "faith failure." Peter's failure, however, is not the final word. There is forgiveness.

The Prayer Life of Jesus

The study of Jesus' prayer life can deepen our own prayer practices. These five sessions examine the importance of prayer at various stages of Jesus' life and ministry. He made no important decisions without consulting God.

Prepare the Way

In these sessions, we will seek to prepare the way toward and into the Christmas season. We begin with the theme of hopeful watchfulness in light of the coming of Christ. Next, we will spend two sessions considering the ministry of John the Baptist, the forerunner of Christ. Then, we will consider Matthew's account of the birth of Jesus and join in wonder at the miracle of "God with us." Finally, we will remember the story of the "holy innocents" killed by Herod in his attempt to eliminate the Christ child's threat to his power.

Proverbs for Living

Long ago, a collection of wise teachers committed themselves to the ways of God and collected this wisdom into what we know as the book of Proverbs. These four lessons explore the simple truth of Proverbs: there is a good life to be had—a life lived in faithfulness to God.

Qualities of Our Missional God

Too often we are tempted to let "numbers" drive missions. The book of Numbers reminds us that missions is motivated by something deeper. Missions reflects the heart and nature of God. If we can just get past the math, we can see God's nature clearly in the book of Numbers. . . in the wilderness.

Responding to the Resurrection

All major events of human history elicit responses as varied as the personalities and situations represented by those affected. No one witnesses a world-changing event without being affected in some way. Studying the response of early followers helps us to shape our own response to the resurrection of Jesus. Each of us must consider our response to Jesus' life, teachings, death, resurrection, and call on our lives.

The Seven Deadly Sins

What exactly is sin? Just as we organize our cupboards and our schedules to make sense of our lives, Christian thinkers have organized sin into a number of categories in order to understand and surrender these patterns to God. The notion of "seven deadly sins" emerged as a way to recognize specific dangers to our spiritual lives. The purpose of the book is to guide people away from sin and into a wise and godly life.

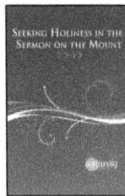

Seeking Holiness in the Sermon on the Mount

The Sermon on the Mount has long been recognized as the pinnacle of Jesus' teaching. But with this importance in mind, it's easy to think of Jesus' teachings as lofty and idealistic, offering little guidance for everyday life. Perhaps Jesus' sermon allows us to see beyond ourselves, beyond our own failures and shortcomings—revealing God's intention for our lives.

Spiritual Disciplines
Obligation or Opportunity?

The spiritual disciplines help deepen a believer's faith and increases his or her intimacy with Christ. In this study, we take a deeper look at some of the disciplines and consider their practice as a response to God's love.

Sing We Now of Christmas

In this study, we will explore some familiar prophecies, as well as the Gospel birth narratives, through the lens of five traditional Christmas carols. As carols have grown to be a fuller and more meaningful part of our worship and celebration, so too can the stories of Jesus' birth continue to grow within us and enrich our faith experience.

Stewardship
A Way of Living

Great News! Stewardship is not about money! At least not *just* about money. Certainly, stewardship relates to money, and, yes, we need to tithe. However, stewardship branches out into multiple areas of life. Properly practiced, this act of service can lead to peace and purpose in living.

The Ten Commandments

When the Ten Commandments are in the news, it is usually because a judge or teacher has hung them up on the walls. The Ten Commandments do not need to be posted or even preached nearly so much as they need to be practiced and viewed as life-giving, joyful affirmations of a better way of life.

War, Peace, and the Bible

As people of faith, we are faced daily with an expectation that we participate in violent actions, our willingness to allow violence in the world to continue, and our response to violence in our lives. Is there a place for war and violence in our faith?

What Would Jesus Say?
A Lenten Study

To address what Jesus would say, we need to discover what Jesus did say. These lessons will attempt to help us understand Jesus' teachings and apply them today.

The Wonder of Easter

In 1 Corinthians 15, Paul asserts that the message that Jesus died for our sins, was buried, and rose on the third day is "of first importance" (v. 3). It is the core of the gospel story and of the Christian faith. But as much as Easter is a mystery to contemplate, it is also a hope to embrace and good news to proclaim.

**NextSunday Studies
are available from**

NextSunday
Resources

www.ingramcontent.com/pod-product-compliance
Lightning Source LLC
Chambersburg PA
CBHW070540030426
42337CB00016B/2284